P9-AOJ-591

378.73
St9

110923

DATE DUE			

DISCARDED

Students
and Their
Institutions

CARL A. RUDISILL LIBRARY
LENOIR RHYNE COLLEGE

Dean of Students

Students and Their Institutions

A Changing Relationship

Edited by
J. W. PELTASON and
MARCY V. MASSENGALE

CARL A. RUDISILL LIBRARY
LENOIR RHYNE COLLEGE

American Council on Education   *Washington, D.C.*

© 1978 by the American Council on Education
One Dupont Circle, Washington, D.C. 20036

378.73
St 9
110923
Sept. 1979

Library of Congress Cataloging in Publication Data
Main entry under title:
Students and their institutions.

     1.   Education, Higher—United States—1965-
—Congresses.   2.   Personnel service in higher
education—United States—Congresses.
I.   Peltason, Jack Walter.   II.   Massengale, Marcy V.
LA227.3.S85   378.73   78-6257
ISBN 0-8268-1393-3

9 8 7 6 5 4 3 2 1

Printed in the United States of America

Contributors

Jerry Apodaca
GOVERNOR, STATE OF NEW MEXICO

Peter D. Bell
SPECIAL ASSISTANT TO THE SECRETARY, AND COORDINATOR
OF THE SPECIAL STUDIES GROUP, DEPARTMENT OF HEALTH,
EDUCATION, AND WELFARE

Ernest L. Boyer
U.S. COMMISSIONER OF EDUCATION

Joseph A. Califano, Jr.
SECRETARY OF HEALTH, EDUCATION, AND WELFARE

Lisle C. Carter, Jr.
PRESIDENT, UNIVERSITY OF THE DISTRICT OF COLUMBIA

Martha E. Church
PRESIDENT, HOOD COLLEGE

John T. Fey
CHAIRMAN, EQUITABLE LIFE ASSURANCE SOCIETY
OF THE UNITED STATES

Bruce Fuller
STAFF DIRECTOR, ASSEMBLY PERMANENT SUBCOMMITTEE
ON POSTSECONDARY EDUCATION, STATE OF CALIFORNIA,
AND STUDENT, STANFORD UNIVERSITY

Stephen H. Fuller
VICE-PRESIDENT, GENERAL MOTORS CORPORATION

David P. Gardner
PRESIDENT, UNIVERSITY OF UTAH

Joseph N. Hankin
PRESIDENT, WESTCHESTER COMMUNITY COLLEGE

Timothy J. Healy, S.J.
PRESIDENT, GEORGETOWN UNIVERSITY

Harold L. Hodgkinson
EXECUTIVE DIRECTOR OF THE PROFESSIONAL INSTITUTE,
AMERICAN MANAGEMENT ASSOCIATIONS

T. Edward Hollander
CHANCELLOR, NEW JERSEY STATE DEPARTMENT
OF EDUCATION

D. Bruce Johnstone
VICE-PRESIDENT FOR ADMINISTRATION,
UNIVERSITY OF PENNSYLVANIA

George O. Klemp, Jr.
DIRECTOR OF ASSESSMENT, MC BER AND COMPANY

Henry M. Levin
PROFESSOR, SCHOOL OF EDUCATION AND DEPARTMENT
OF ECONOMICS, STANFORD UNIVERSITY

Michael Liethen
GENERAL COUNSEL, UNIVERSITY OF WISCONSIN—MADISON

James E. Nelson
VICE PRESIDENT, PROGRAM PLANNING AND RESEARCH,
COLLEGE ENTRANCE EXAMINATION BOARD

Joel Packer
LEGISLATIVE DIRECTOR, NATIONAL STUDENT LOBBY

Robert L. Payton
PRESIDENT, EXXON EDUCATION FOUNDATION

Susan Rink, B.V.M.
PRESIDENT, MUNDELEIN COLLEGE

John R. Silber
PRESIDENT, BOSTON UNIVERSITY

Hayden W. Smith
VICE PRESIDENT FOR RESEARCH, COUNCIL FOR FINANCIAL
AID TO EDUCATION

Stuart A. Taylor
DIRECTOR OF TRAINING AND DEVELOPMENT,
TEXTRON, INC.

Patricia A. Watson
DIRECTOR OF ACADEMIC SERVICES,
UNIVERSITY OF SAN DIEGO

Preface

"THINGS" NEVER STAY THE SAME, and they do not change very much either. But all involved with higher education know that life on the campus in the seventies is different from life in the sixties. Protests, once a way of life, are now an occasional event (perhaps more occasional than some would have it), but a state of siege is no longer the normal condition for the president's office. By act of Congress and constitutional amendment, those over eighteen are sufficiently adult to be voting citizens, thus ending what the returning veterans of World War II started; the university is no longer in loco parentis. If we provide for students all the services that some of their leaders seem to demand, however, we are fast on the way to becoming in loco grandparentis.

There have been more changes, to cite just a few: Students appear to be more career-minded. The notion of students as customers—although we keep insisting that they are clients—has taken hold, bringing with it requirements for institutions to observe "fair practices." The enormous drive to equalize opportunities has resulted in larger numbers of minorities and low-income students on our campuses and in the movement of women into programs heretofore thought to be for men only. And as the number of traditional-age undergraduates and degree-bound graduates has leveled off, the word "student" no longer describes only the young. The goal of lifelong learning has assumed significance.

Many pressures impinge on the time and energy of university and college administrators who must comply, or at least try to comply, with a confusing welter of government regulations, struggle with budgets, satisfy the faculty, and interact with the community. And occupying much of the administrator's calendar are concerns about students. Are we listening to them? Do we have the wisdom to distinguish between what students *want* and what they *need*? Do the arrangements for student leadership provide us with the diverse views of the many different kinds of students who are involved in our institutions? Are students getting the kinds of information and advice they need to make decisions about financial arrangements, fields of study, job options, and life goals?

To these ends, the American Council on Education, in its sixtieth Annual Meeting, held in Washington, D.C., October 12–14, 1977, sought to reaffirm one of higher education's principal goals—educating students—by discussing a variety of areas directly related to this goal. The Council publishes this volume of papers from the meeting in the hope that the exchange of ideas herein will spark a new dedication to that goal as well as provide a new impetus to reach it. John F. Hughes and Donna C. Phillips directed and coordinated the plans and programs of the meeting. The Council is indebted to the contributors to this book and to the staff members who helped prepare for and carry out this Annual Meeting of the American Council on Education.

J. W. PELTASON

MARCY V. MASSENGALE

Contents

ix

The Changing World and Higher Education

ERNEST L. BOYER

TWENTY YEARS AGO, the attention of the world was riveted on a one-hundred-eighty-four-pound object in the sky. The Soviets had electrified this planet by putting *Sputnik* into orbit; Americans, especially, were both angry and afraid. If a satellite could be lifted into space, what more lethal object might be targeted toward our continent here on earth?

At that time, one issue seemed absolutely clear. Somehow, every one agreed, a direct link existed between education and the world's first satellite. President Eisenhower declared that "young people now in college must be equipped to live in an age of intercontinental ballistic missiles." James B. Conant warned:

> Many people are quite unconscious of the relation between high school education and the welfare of the United States. They are still living in imagination in a world which knew neither nuclear weapons nor Soviet imperialism.

America's response to *Sputnik* was urgent and specific. The National Defense Education Act was passed by Congress to support the education and employment of teachers of sciences, mathematics, and foreign languages. The Conant Report called for special programs for the gifted student. Curricular reform exploded everywhere resulting in the "new" math, the "new" physics, the "new" biology. The National Science Foundation grew and supported science departments and young talent in the schools. In short, American education moved forward with great imagination to meet the challenge of *Sputnik*.

Twenty years have passed since *Sputnik,* and today a new, more subtle urgency exists regarding American education. The conviction is

1

growing that we must once again reform our colleges and schools while still holding to the deeply cherished essentials of academic life. The country's changing social context and changing students are important factors in this move to reform. Educators at all levels must respond to these changes in three crucial areas.

A closer relationship

Education must become more coordinated. The relationship between our colleges and schools must become closer.

More than fifty years ago, Henry Clinton Morrison observed that

> as a people, we do not think in terms of schools. We have no educational system; we have an elementary school, a high school, and a college.

A layer-cake approach to education perhaps made sense fifty years ago. At that time, each academic level had a special mission, and each institution served its own special group of students. In 1920, for example, most young Americans had what was called a grade school education. Only 20 percent of our teenagers went on to secondary school. Only 15 percent of high school graduates went on to college.

Then, the elementary school, the high school, and the college had separate and unique jobs to do. Only a very narrow band of students moved along the academic spectrum. The majority of young people were turned away from educational opportunity by artificial barriers of class, race, and sex, and our advanced schools and colleges could carry on their work in splendid isolation. But for several decades now, the student population has shifted dramatically, and isolation will no longer do. In 1918, after World War I, a National Education Association report called for universal secondary education. The objective was to teach "democracy" and "citizenship" and to educate the children of all immigrants.

The effect of this new vision was significant. In 1930, 50 percent of the nation's youth were enrolled in secondary school. The figure rose to 76 percent in 1950. By 1970, over 92 percent of America's teenagers were high school students. After World War II, a shift occurred in the student population at the higher education level. GI's, many of whose parents never went to college, came to campuses formerly ruled off limits. Once they had enrolled, they found that they could excel academically. The push for open access was moving upward.

In 1940, before World War II, 35.7 percent of America's high school graduates went on to college. The figure increased to 42.7 percent in 1950, and in 1960 it had moved to almost 50 percent. At long last, America had committed itself to equal educational opportunity. The artificial education barriers had been broken. The majority of our students—not just the privileged few—were going on to high school and then on to college.

Here is the crucial point: after World War II, for the first time in our history, educators at all levels shared a vision and were called upon to serve the same group of students. Yet, the structure of our schools never quite caught up with the social reality. Educators continued to operate our schools and colleges as if they were unrelated to each other.

Today those structural distances still persist. Elementary and high school teachers infrequently meet together. College administrators rarely sit down with their counterparts in secondary schools. University administrators set admission standards without consulting their colleagues in the schools.

The time has come for educators from all levels to focus increasingly on education, rather than on their separate institutions. It is time to recognize that while school and college administrators may survive the Rube Goldberg approach to planning, the students are the ones who face the resulting curricular gaps and overlaps. The students are the ones who are caught in the academic cul de sac. Clearly, the bigness of the education job requires that we engage occasionally at least in interlevel planning.

In 1945, Harvard University produced its now famous general education report, commonly called the "Redbook." The nations had been devastated by a terrible war, and the "Redbook" called for a general education curriculum to help rebuild a shattered world. Colleges and universities all across the country copied Harvard's reform proposals, which, incidentally, the Harvard faculty did not adopt.

What is less well remembered about the report is that more than half of it discussed not the collegiate course of study, but the secondary school curriculum. Its authors recognized that it is irresponsible to purpose curricular reform in higher education without looking at the secondary school as well.

A lack of coordination

Before the turn of this century, higher education leaders were troubled by the lack of coordination between the elementary school, the high school, and the college. Educators at each level were charging off independently, adding years of study to their programs and designing curriculum on their own. Led by Charles Eliot of Harvard, these educators formed a committee, composed of school and college representatives, to look at education from the early years to college, to build a better academic sequence.

Such leadership is required again. Needed now is a group of elementary, secondary, and higher education leaders, joined by citizens and teachers, to examine the total academic situation, including some very basic questions.

1. How can we teach the basic skills?

2. How can the junior high school provide smooth transition between the lower and the upper grades?

3. How can the senior high school provide more educational options while still promoting excellence?

4. How can the high school and the college general education curriculum be more sharply focused and more fully integrated?

5. How can colleges and universities serve more effectively the older student?

The panel's goal would not be to dominate educator's actions, but to be supportive and to promote the recognition that educators should serve students, not institutions. Sharing resources and developing common strategies will enable education in America to achieve the excellence we all desire.

A requirement for flexibility

The changes in the social context of America and in the student population require that education become more flexible in calendar and location. During most of our academic history, schools and colleges were constructed for the very young. Classes were scheduled to coincide with the work week. Students were expected to pursue their studies, full time, before entering the "real world." To be a "dropout" was a social stigma, a label to be avoided at all cost.

Now, these requirements have begun to loosen; the implications for education are enormous. First, America's demographic profile has shifted dramatically; the so-called baby boom has now become an "adult-age bulge." In this decade alone, the number of Americans in the fifty–fifty-nine-age bracket will rise by 17 percent, in the older-than-60 group, by 35 percent.

During the past fifty years, there have also been dramatic changes among the nation's youth. Teenagers now mature physically two full years earlier than their grandparents did. One young wit has noted, if Booth Tarkington were writing *Seventeen* today, he would have to title it *Fifteen* because the characteristics he described now appear much earlier than before. To add to the confusion, the well-ordered adult world is changing. The average American work week is thirty-six and a half hours, down from forty-three hours in 1945 and sixty-two hours in 1900.

The number of older students going on to college continues to increase. Today, approximately one-third of our college students are twenty-five years of age or older, and more than 50 percent attend part time. Not only has the student age pattern begun to change, but the location of learning has also shifted. When I was young, there was no television in our home. I was twelve years old before we purchased our first radio. We did receive a daily newspaper and the *National Geographic,* which I eagerly devoured as soon as it arrived. Our Model A took us on short excursions, rarely over one hundred miles, from our Ohio home.

In those years, school was the central learning place. The teacher —for better or for worse—was the key source of knowledge, and the classroom was the intellectual window to the world. (It was only later that I learned just how clouded that window could sometimes be.)

Today that world I knew is ancient history. Young children, two to five years old, now watch television over four hours a day, nearly thirty hours every week; that is over 1,500 hours every year. By the time a youngster enters first grade, he or she has had 6,000 hours of television viewing.

Television saturation continues after school begins and very often the traditional source of information—the teacher—has been bypassed. Several years ago, our young son, who had just entered kindergarten, said the alphabet one night when he went to bed, rather than his prayers. When he finished, I complimented him for having recited the alphabet without a hitch, even though he had been in kindergarten just one week. "Actually," he replied, "I learned the alphabet on 'Sesame Street,' but my kindergarten teacher thinks she taught it to me." I was delighted: my son had not only learned the alphabet but he had also learned the system, too!

Whatever else we may think of our new electronic world, it does seem to stimulate a sense of community, despite the radio's disembodied voices and the detached and artificial images of the screen. But, as John Platt of the University of California reminded us, these images and voices

> represent a world larger and older than the family or the village night —stretching to Washington or to the moon—or years into the vanished past. And with habit, they become more real and more important than the family, as the war comes nightly to our dinner table and we all walk on the moon together or attend the Kennedy funeral.

Students are learning outside the classroom in other ways as well.

Opening new worlds

My *National Geographic,* which gave me glimpses of the outside world, has today been smothered by an avalanche of publications— some good, some bad—which open up new worlds to students. In 1948, the year Harry Truman defeated Dewey, the *New York Times* index ran 1,211 pages. By 1970, the total had soared to 2,291 pages. Over 2,000 large, closely printed pages are now required merely to list by author, title, and subject the paperback books currently in print. Paperbacks, magazines, television, and travel now compete equally with the classroom and the textbook for students' attention.

Today, for better or for worse, Archie Bunker is better known than Silas Marner; Fellini is more influential than Faulkner; and the six o'clock news is more compelling than the history text.

What is the contemporary educator to make of this situation? In the days ahead, colleges and universities will not only have students of many different ages coming back to campus; there will also be campuses in many different places. Increasingly, business, industry, and governments will give their employees time off to go back to college. More classes will be held in the buildings where the people work. A greater number of mature students will be engaged in independent study.

During the coming decade, formal education also will increasingly be linked to television, to the library, and to travel. Educators will begin to use these other learning resources as supplements to the classroom, viewing them as enrichments rather than as threats.

Consequently, our schools and colleges, while protecting their intellectual freedom, cannot stand alone. These other institutions are woven into the social fabric of the nation; the academic community must engage them in the job of educating our citizens.

American education can modify its academic schedules. It can expand the campus to meet the changing needs of students. It can enrich the classroom and the book, while still promoting academic excellence.

The purpose of education

The purpose of education is the third area that educators must address in the light of the many changes that have occurred in American society.

When *Sputnik* was fired into space twenty years ago, our educational purposes—for one fleeting moment—seemed clear.

The Air Force Chief of Staff said, "The security of our Nation . . . depends as much on the wisdom and skill of our engineers, scientists, and technicians as it does upon the courage of our fighting men." Franklin Murphy, Chancellor of the University of Kansas, said, "The message which this little ball carries to Americans, if they would but stop and listen, is that in the last . . . half of the 20th Century, nothing is as important as the trained and educated mind."

The goal was to train the scientists, technicians, and engineers required to move America more effectively into the space age.

But today, that purpose has been achieved. American educators now are groping for a more enduring, a more fundamental mission.

In one sense, American education has a common goal today— serving fully the individual differences of students.

This goal is valid. We must continue to expand access to our colleges and schools. We must overcome in our schools and colleges the racial prejudices, the sexual stereotypes, and the insensitivities toward the handicapped that exist. We must recognize the uniqueness of every student. We must push for creativity, not conformity, on the campus.

But access reflects the means of education, not its end. Once the school door has been opened to all students, a nagging question remains, Does education have a larger social purpose to fulfill? Specifically, do educators have a clear vision of what it means to be an "educated person"?

A recent *Psychology Today* article on the "new mood on campus" suggested that colleges at their very best should be more than a gathering place for isolated learners. It was reported that students—some, at least—expect colleges to have purposes of their own and believe that a core curriculum would improve the current course "hodge-podge."

A curriculum with no common core, no central thrust, is just as flawed as one that is rigid. A college that has no conviction about the goals of education reflects not progress, but a loss of nerve. It is just as wrong to teach that people have no individual differences as it is to teach that they have no things in common.

Not every school or college should declare a single creed or a rigid set of courses: we have had too much carbon-copy thinking in the past. But educators and citizens should begin to search together for a new core of study which draws upon the traditional and emerging academic disciplines to focus on those experiences we share. A readiness for such a quest exists. Even the proponents of the back-to-basics movement seek a closer relationship between what educators teach and the nation's broader social goals.

A revolution of perspective

In 1957, we all stood on earth and watched a satellite hurtling through space. Our perspective was revolutionized. We felt differently about each other and about our future.

Now, two decades later, again we watch a small and fragile object out in space. This time, through television, as we look back upon ourselves, the silver ball we see is Spaceship Earth. Once again our perspective has been changed. From this more sobering vantage, the old artificial barriers to perceiving the similarities of the earth's peoples are less visible. Our new perspective is both more personal and more global.

From this perspective, we confront more fundamental questions: Where will we get our food, and how can it be distributed appropriately? What is the extent of our energy supply, and how can it be shared equitably? How can we reduce the poisons in the atmosphere? Can we maintain a balance between population and the life support system of this planet? These are a few of the transcendent issues that today's young people—and all of us—must begin to think and talk about carefully. Several years ago, at a seminar in the ancient Persian city of Persepolis, John Gardner said:

> Our planet is but a speck of dust in the universe, and our life on it is but an instant in the long stretch of astrophysical time. Still, it is the only planet we have, and our life on it holds great possibilities

of beauty and dignity and meaning. Yet if it were asked of us how we spend our instant of time on our speck of dust, we would have to say, "We spend a good deal of it fighting one another and laying waste our earth."

"Surely," Gardner continued, "all of us here believe that we can do better."

I believe that our schools and colleges will, as they have always done, adjust themselves responsibly to the changing conditions of our world and will educate our students to live with both civility and constraint.

The Era of Engagement

JOSEPH A. CALIFANO, JR.

Two EVENTS OCCURRED twenty years ago that had a profound effect on education in America: the vaulting into space of the Soviet satellite, *Sputnik,* and the civil rights movement, whose greatest force and national impact date back to Martin Luther King's bus boycott in Montgomery, Alabama, in 1956.

Neither of those events took place in the world of education. Yet, just as *Sputnik* riveted our attention dramatically on the issue of quality in American education, the civil rights movement forced us to confront the issue of equality in American education. In the ensuing twenty years, the story of American higher education has been a story of our efforts to honor both those fundamental values: excellence and equality.

Since 1957, federal support for higher education has grown spectacularly. In 1960, federal spending for higher education totaled only $1 billion. By 1966, federal spending had grown to $2.9 billion; by 1976, it had grown to $14 billion. As federal support for higher education grew, the number and variety of educational institutions grew. In 1960, the United States had 521 community colleges with a student population of 451,000. Only ten years later, the number of community colleges had grown to 827—an increase of more than 60 percent in a decade—and their student population had almost quadrupled to 1,630,000. For higher education generally, the number of college students grew from 3.6 million in 1960 to nearly 12 million in 1976. In those 16 years, the percentage of high school graduates entering college rose dramatically—from 32 percent in 1960 to 45 percent in 1976. With this growth came what may be the most important development of all: a dramatic change in the social composition of the student body. One fact tells the story: By 1973, more than 60 percent of all college students came from families in which the head of the household had not completed even one year of college. The children of black, poor, and blue-collar families began to join the children of the elite in our colleges and universities. More women aspired to and gained precious positions in our elite graduate schools, particularly in law.

The new immigrants

This change and growth in higher education represent the greatest assimilation of a group of people into educated society in the history of civilization. For these millions of college graduates are the new immigrants—seeking a new land of opportunity and fulfillment. This great movement has not been heralded, but it dwarfs the Manhattan Project; it even surpasses our national effort to land men on the moon. No technological achievement, however complex and sophisticated, could match this feat of educating and uplifting the human mind and spirit.

This achievement is a tribute to the capacity and energy of the higher education community which responded creatively, sensitively, and efficiently to the demands of social change in America.

In an era of political disillusion, moral confusion, and hypercriticism in America, it is useful to underscore these events. For at a time when critics were charging that our institutions were hide-bound, unresponsive, and obsolete, our institutions of government and education were responding to a growth in demand for higher education unprecedented in our history.

For the higher education community, the era that dawned with *Sputnik* and the civil rights movement—an era that continues to this day—may rightly be called the Era of Engagement. That era has caused some headaches for the higher education community and the nation. The Era of Engagement has been crowded, noisy, expensive, and tumultuous, but Americans can be proud of the way higher education has met the challenge. It is important, however, that we not congratulate ourselves prematurely.

It is true that in the ten years from 1965 to 1975, we more than doubled the percentage of blacks between eighteen and twenty-four years old who were students in college—from 10 to 21 percent. That is a striking achievement. But it is also true that in 1975, fewer than four of every one hundred new Ph.D.'s were black. In fact, a leading black ecnomist tells us

> If American colleges and universities were to hire every Black Ph.D. in the United States, active or retired (or indeed, living or dead)— a 100 percent drain from industry, government, and other institutions—the result would still be less than three Black faculty members per institution.

Clearly, we can do better in broadening access to higher education in America. If we can, we must, not only for black and minority students, but also for the handicapped, for women, and for other disadvantaged groups.

Higher education has made progress, both in opening opportunities for women in America and in changing attitudes toward their role. But the fact remains that, in most academic disciplines, the absence of women is a continuing scandal. Women faculty members too often receive less pay, are locked out of tenure, and are bunched in the lower faculty echelons. Most ominously, the percentage of women faculty members dwindled from 22.5 percent in 1974–75 to 21.7 percent in 1975–76.

I am committed, and this administration is committed, to the principles of equal opportunity in Title IX of the Education Amendments of 1972. Affirmative action to give life and force to those principles is a challenge to our institutions of higher education and an opportunity for them, in athletics as well as academics.

Many colleges have responded aggressively and creatively to the academic and legal imperative for more women in the classroom— as teachers and as students. The clock is now running on a new and perhaps even more difficult challenge for equal opportunity: intercollegiate athletics. The athletic adjustment period under Title IX draws to a close in less than a year. The cooperation and leadership of the higher education community is essential if we are to make Title IX a reality in athletic and academic areas. The leaders of the country's colleges and universities must bring to bear on the thorny and emotional issue of women in athletics the same leadership that has opened the nation's campuses to so many minorities and disadvantaged Americans. Title IX is the law of the land, it must be enforced. The more creative and innovative educators are in fulfilling the law, the less intrusive and cumbersome government has to be.

Access for the handicapped

Continuing the Era of Engagement in higher education will also mean broader access for handicapped students. The world of the handicapped, in education as in every other sector of American life, is a world of barriers: admissions barriers, attitudinal barriers, architectural barriers.

The regulations HEW has issued to implement section 504 of the Rehabilitation Act of 1973 forbid all institutions receiving federal funds from discriminating against the handicapped—in admissions, in hiring, in physical access, and in academic programs. The handicapped will have significant impact on higher education institutions. Their presence will require changes that are worth the effort.

The government intends to give colleges and universities maximum help as they work to comply with the law. In cooperation with the American Council on Education, the U.S. Department of Health, Education, and Welfare has made several grants under the new HEATH Project (Higher Education and the Handicapped) to help academic institutions come into compliance as smoothly as possible.

Broadening opportunity in American education and in our national life has not been easy. It will never be easy. It is proving even more complex and turbulent to open the doors of higher education to blacks, Hispanics, or women, at City College of New York or the Davis Medical School (University of California) or the University of Arkansas than it was to assimilate the Jews and Italians through the lower East Side of New York or the Puerto Ricans through the West Bronx. But the ideal of full opportunity is even more worthwhile and exciting for our colleges today than it was for the leaders of New York City eighty years ago.

Broadening access to higher education will be a preoccupation of the higher education community and government for years to come. But it cannot be our only concern: there are other pressing engagements that we must be about.

These new engagements fall into two categories: first, engagement in the community; second, engagement with still more new student groups.

Improving secondary education

Deeper engagement in the community may be both the most difficult and ultimately the most rewarding for our society. Especially important is the need for institutions of higher learning to involve themselves in improving secondary education.

This nation's secondary schools are, literally and figuratively, fighting for their lives. While some of them are coping effectively with their problems, many—especially in our largest cities—are a shambles. Even the best have serious questions about what their purposes should be.

If they are to recapture their authority and relevance, these schools need help in innovating. Members of the higher education community who have faced large problems and coped successfully with them are in a position to help in several possible ways.

For example, colleges and universities could establish imaginative relationships with secondary schools—links that benefit both.

There are, in many of our cities, new "magnet schools" for students with special interests in the arts, in business education, in allied health professions training; academically intensive schools for especially gifted students. There is a clear opportunity for colleges and universities to help these innovative institutions survive and succeed. For example, Harvard has allied itself with a school in Boston to help its students and teachers in dozens of ways.

Other schools are experimenting with ways to relate education to the world of work. They are helping young people find ways of alternating work and schooling without suffering the stigma of being called "dropouts." Today, at many higher education institutions, it is possible for a college student to leave, work for a year, and return to the campus. But our secondary schools do not offer such flexibility. The higher education community, with all its experience in alternating work and study, could lend a hand to this movement to give greater flexibility to high schools and their students. One way is to give life-experience credit to young people as well as to older citizens who embark upon higher education.

Other links between higher and secondary education suggest themselves: arts programs that involve both college and secondary students; faculty exchanges; college programs for gifted high school students; programs of continuing education for teachers.

The second new engagement for higher education—finding and serving new groups of students—is one that many colleges and universities have embraced with excellent results for themselves and the communities they serve.

The College of New Rochelle is an excellent example. Once a quiet, Catholic-supported college for women, New Rochelle is now a lively, multicampus center that touches all sorts of people's lives.

Faced with declining enrollments and growing costs, the college survived by reaching out through its new School of New Resources to retired people, to urban dwellers in a labor union higher education program, and to adults living in a vast urban apartment complex. Today, the college is planning to establish a new center of higher education in the aching heart of the bombed-out, burnt-out community of the South Bronx.

HEW intends to give all the help it can to this courageous initiative. For it is by such heroic engagements that institutions renew themselves and the lives of ever more people.

The Era of Engagement in the recent past has meant moving more and more people into our colleges and universities. For the future, it also means moving our colleges and universities ever closer to our people, where they live.

A greater fear

There may be those people who, confronted with the myriad concerns and goals for American education, will fear that the challenge is too great. But the greater fear is that American higher education, with all its power and promise, may attempt too little.

We have set for ourselves in America some rigorous goals for our system of education: to transmit the values of democracy; to assimilate group after group of Americans who were once shut out; to train the professionals who will guide our institutions, make our scientific advances, create our works of art. In all these ambitious efforts, we have succeeded more often than we have fallen short.

Stephen Bailey wrote for the nation's Bicentennial a wise book entitled *The Purposes of Education* (Bloomington, Ind.: Phi Delta Kappa, 1976). In it, he reminds us that we are the only nation whose written charter exhorts its people to "the pursuit of happiness." He underscores the fact that education is interwoven with that pursuit.

No major institution in our society means more to our national pursuit of happiness, of fulfillment, of economic and social well-being than the university.

Education is to a democratic society what prayer is to a monastic order. To teach in a free society is to be entrusted with the mind and heart of the future. To be a leader of higher education in the most educated nation in recorded history is to hold the keys to the kingdom of opportunity. But to be an engaged leader of higher education is to give those keys freely so that every talent can find fulfillment.

The Public and the University:
A Decade of Difficulty

JERRY APODACA

DURING THE PERIOD OF UNREST on the nation's college and university campuses ten years ago, the institutions and its people were highly esteemed by the public. It was the restless young who were targeted for the outrage of their elders. Every parent's dream was to see his or her child with a degree and unlimited prospects for a successful career. They were mystified by and resentful of their children's lack of appreciation for a college education or a seemingly inexhaustible supply of material goods, neither of which was available to older generations.

Then, an unsophisticated society perhaps overrated the economic value of a college degree.

Today, critics are once again challenging higher education, and the target has shifted. Unlike the critics of higher education of the sixties, today's are moving against the institutions. Much more sophisticated than the criticis of ten years ago, they are willing to do battle in the arenas of public opinion, government, and the courts. If their criticisms gather force, the higher education community and the country's leaders have only themselves to blame. We did not do enough to warn the nation that, if a baccalaureate degree became a common credential, its intrinsic economic value would diminish.

This observation is not against an educated society. But we should have been more candid in predicting the benefits of a college education. We should have been talking more forcefully about the many reasons for a college education not at all related to employment.

However, in the scramble for more students and programs, we chose to be mute on this issue when it suited our purposes. The American people today realize, although we should have made them understand before now, that for many students a two-year vocational program may be better for their job objectives than a graduate degree, that an individual's hopes may not be satisfied by the mere acquisition of a degree or even by four years of higher learning.

This sudden and bitter realization may indeed cause a backlash of education consumers against higher education that may be even more severe than that confronting primary and secondary public education. Unfortunately for the higher education community, the pendulum of human emotion and reaction does not cease until it has run its full course and generates an opposite reaction.

A decade of difficulty

A decade of some hostility, accusation, and difficulty may be in store for the universities. Dollars will continue to be a problem. Postsecondary education is a labor-intensive industry, highly dependent on individual faculty working with limited groups of students. As inflation and salary requirements increase, so will the demands for greater state and federal support.

Higher education surely holds a high place in the present Administration's priorities, but other activities will be competing with higher education for government support. Within the U.S. Department of Health, Education, and Welfare, the greatest interest appears to be in income maintenance, welfare, and health care reform initiatives.

Another possible reason for any apparent lack of interest in higher education is more hopeful: in comparison with health care, welfare, energy, and other national issues, educational services are now considered to be of high quality. This suggestion offers little consolation to those in the academic community who will be engaged in a revolution of rising, then frustrated expectations.

The greatest growth area in education seems to be at the community college level. A number of competing groups will be interested in serving the so-called nontraditional students—older persons seeking delayed education or a second career.

Probably, public colleges and universities will not, and do not need to, grow significantly in the years ahead. With declining or static enrollments, the emphasis should be on renovation and replacement of facilities rather than on vast development and expansion. Citizens will not likely support any course for higher education that requires enormous sums of money.

Higher education institutions will have to learn to tighten belts as they are scrutinized increasingly. People feel they have been on the outside looking in, their noses pressed against the window, while important decision-makers—the politicians, the teachers, the faculty and administrators—concern themselves only with the players on the inside.

Although this message is somber, the higher education community should not be disheartened. Many of the current academic programs may have to be reexamined, including those which were added to curricula in response to the sixties' catchword, "relevance." The array of programs available to students must constantly change to meet the demands of a world in which change is the only constant. But in doing so, one thing must never change—a dedication to excellence.

Articulating the need for excellence

Quality education should not be surrendered for any reason. Scholarship and excellence must be realistic goals of the university experience, even if they cannot be perfectly achieved in a world of limited human beings. The university must not become a multimillion dollar extension of high school. It is up to the higher education community to articulate the need for excellence—forcefully, cogently, persuasively—in the face of government regulations, public apathy, criticism, and legislative disinterest.

Higher education must adjust to a world that will demand new things of it. But if there ever is to exist a haven for a spirited discussion of goals and free-wheeling debate on the future of education or the problems of society, it must be the university campus.

The new era of questioning and the public's discontent over the substantial investments it makes into higher education should not be feared, but welcomed. All citizens must also understand, and educators and administrators are the only ones who can make them understand, that even more than a public facility or a location, a university is a spirit, a set of circumstances in which scholars and teachers are engaged in evaluating and passing on the heritage of the past and in disseminating current knowledge. A great university, in the words of a retired University of New Mexico professor, exists anywhere faculty and students enjoy

> the freedom to pursue their own search for knowledge and truth, freedom to question, freedom to decide for themselves and to profess to all their individual positions on philosophical, social, political and economic issues, freedom to be wrong without undue penalty, and freedom to propose and implement new and different solutions to problems facing the human race.

All faculty and administrators want to mold their institutions into greatness. It will be difficult to encourage the self-examination, the dissent, the sometimes bitter debate on campus required to achieve greatness, especially when the outside world will also be questioning the institution's performance and motivation. But such examination must be done.

Worthwhile goals are nearly always difficult to realize. The country will be much better if the higher education community pursues its course with strength and grace under scrutiny.

The Cost of a College Education: Getting the Word Out

JAMES E. NELSON

EVERYONE KNOWS THAT IT TAKES MONEY to pursue a postsecondary education. Everyone also knows that giving students financial aid is one of the best ways to achieve access and choice. Christopher Jencks neatly summarizes the role of financial aid in furthering educational equality when he notes, "while lack of money is by no means the most serious problem confronting children from the lower strata seeking education . . . it is the most commonly discussed, the most easily analyzed, and the most readily eliminated."[1]

Most discussions, analyses, and plans for eliminating the financial barrier forget that information about college costs and financial aid is as important as the aid itself. If students and their parents think they cannot afford postsecondary education, they do not even bother to apply. The price tag of education frightens many people away, and the usual rhetoric about "available financial aid" does little to convince them that they can afford the real costs of college. Better information about the actual financial burden of a college education has become a critical need in recent years. And considerable attention will have to be devoted to this issue before it is fully and productively resolved.

Section 493A of the Higher Education Amendments of 1976, proposed by Senator Jacob Javits, requires that academic institutions receiving federal funds make information on costs and aid available to prospective and current students. But the federal interest in this area predates the "Javits language." In 1975 the Fund for the Improvement of Postsecondary Education (FIPSE) funded a national task force,

1. Christopher Jencks, "Social Stratification and Higher Education," in *Financing Higher Education: Alternatives for the Federal Government,* ed. M. D. Orwig (Iowa City: American College Testing Program, 1971), p. 88.

Better Information for Student Choice (BISC). The task force demonstrated that institutions could voluntarily provide the kind of improved information services to students that the Javits language requires.

This paper is largely an outgrowth of the College Entrance Examination Board's participation in the BISC task force. The College Board project, under the direction of William D. Van Dusen, focused on the issue of better information about costs and student aid, seeking specifically to learn what kinds of misinformation people have about the costs of postsecondary education, why better information is not provided, and how the situation can be improved.[2] Helping the College Board in this investigation were Barat College, Macomb Community College, Mountain Empire Community College, Oberlin College, Pasadena City College, Portland State University, University of California at Irvine, University of Massachusetts at Amherst, Ventura College, and the National Student Education Fund.

Misinformation and its consequences

The College Board study revealed widespread misinformation about college costs and financial aid. For instance, a 1975 study in Iowa found that high school seniors planning to attend particular colleges thought that the costs would be 55 percent lower than the financial aid officers at the same institutions said they were.[3] A national survey of high school juniors showed that many had downgraded their college plans because they thought they could not afford to attend the type of institution they preferred.[4] In the National Longitudinal Study, the reason given by one-third of the high school seniors who did not continue their education was that they believed they could not afford it.[5] According to other estimates, the proportion of young people who do not go to college for financial reasons may be as high as 50 percent.[6] Data from numerous statewide studies indicate that,

2. W. D. Van Dusen and J. E. Nelson, *Making It Count: A Report on a Project to Provide Better Financial Aid Information to Students* (New York: College Entrance Examination Board, 1977).

3. *A Survey of Plans for Education and Careers: A View of What the Iowa High School Senior Class of 1975 Plans to Do Following Graduation and Why* (Evanston, Ill.: College Entrance Examination Board, 1975).

4. J. S. Davis and W. D. Van Dusen, *A Survey of Student Values and Choices* (Atlanta, Ga.: College Entrance Examination Board, 1975).

5. Bruce W. Thompson, *National Longitudinal Study of the High School Class of 1972* (Washington: U.S. Government Printing Office, 1974).

6. W. D. Van Dusen, "Financial Aid and Student Consumerism," paper presented at the Irvine Student Consumerism Conference, University of California at Irvine, December 1, 1976.

even among students already enrolled in postsecondary education, many who may be supposed to have financial need do not apply for available aid, presumably because of lack of information.

What parents think about postsecondary education is important in determining whether their children will seek it out, and this is especially true among lower-income nonwhite families.[7] But little information exists on what parents know about cost and aid, and even less on what they would like to know. The only large-scale study of parental information and misinformation uncovered by the College Board was done in 1965; it showed that at that time parents underestimated the costs of postsecondary education and overestimated their children's chances of receiving financial assistance.[8]

As part of the FIPSE project, the information needs of students were assessed in a number of ways. Other participants in the project found that, regardless of type of student or type of institution, the need for information about costs and financial aid ranked among the top three needs. The College Board assessment focused more directly on the ways in which more specific cost and aid information would influence postsecondary plans and on the kinds of specific information that would be most useful to students.

All our student respondents planned on some form of postsecondary education. Nearly six in ten, however, believed that, if they had more cost and aid information about postsecondary opportunities, they would change their minds about the kind of institution they would attend. This belief was not limited to low-income students; 38 percent of those from upper-income families and 57 percent of those from middle-income families said that, given better information, their decisions might be different. Nearly four in ten of the respondents planned to attend a public two-year college; over half of that group said they would prefer to attend a four-year college if cost were not a factor.

The respondents were interested in almost any kind of information, but most important to them was information on the timing and manner of payment of college costs, on the total cost of the degree program until graduation, and on the probability of changes in cost

7. A. H. Kirshner and J. S. Davis, *The Ways and Means: A Study of the Needs and Resources of Students Enrolled in UNCF Member Institutions,* Research Report, Vol. 2, No. 1 (New York: United Negro College Fund, June 1977).

8. B. L. N. Marple and W. E. Marple, "How Affluent Families Plan to Pay for College," *College Board Review,* Spring 1967, p. 28.

from year to year. Also ranked as very important were detailed descriptions of the kinds of aid available, information on the kind of aid that goes to students like themselves, and specific facts about available jobs, application deadlines and procedures, and loan repayment procedures. And the respondents believed that these kinds of information were not readily available from postsecondary institutions.

Reasons for the lack of information

The College Board study advisory committee concluded that the lack of information about college cost and financial aid could be explained by four major factors.

First, some institutions withheld information because they believed that "the truth will scare students away." Our study confirmed that young people were indeed looking elsewhere, but simply because they could not get the information they needed to make informed decisions about attending these institutions.

The second reason given for the lack of information about costs and aid was "it's too complicated to be truthfully communicated." Obviously, a major problem is that the complexity of the financial aid process makes it difficult for the institution to communicate responsibly. Those who cited complexity as an explanation were correct in their identification of the problem, but their solution—not to communicate at all—was unsatisfactory.

A third reason, most frequently mentioned by public, open-door institutions, was "we couldn't handle any more students than we have now." These institutions simply did not bother to communicate. Their motive, in some cases stated openly, was to discourage needy students from applying for the financial aid they would need in order to attend.

Finally, the policies of some institutions were so unclear that they could not be communicated to others. The very complexity of the application and award procedures served to shield them from public scrutiny.

Improving communication

The institutional participants in the College Board project were not without sympathy for those institutions giving the aforementioned explanations for their failure to communicate. High costs do scare prospective students away. Honest communications do take work and money. Some institutions do have to limit enrollment. Some do not have carefully articulated policies and procedures. Nonetheless, non-communication is not a solution. The project participants believed that it is the institution's responsibility to provide full, honest, and accurate disclosure of both facts and processes; conversely, it is the prospective student's right to receive such information. A basic premise of the study was that postsecondary institutions have the primary responsibility for providing information which will facilitate comparisons among institutions. Moreover, the provision of such information is not only in the student's interest but also in the institution's self-interest, insofar as it helps to attract and hold students.

The disclosures mandated by the Javits language will probably suffice to eliminate whatever fraud and poor practices exist. But they are not adequate to permit the comparisons necessary if students are to have real equality of access and choice. One outcome of the College Board project was the development of a model "Student Financial Aid Cost and Policy" statement, which provides detailed information about student expense budgets, the aid received by students in the preceding year, and the policies under which the institution grants aid. The statement was designed to meet the information needs of students rather than to suit the convenience of the administrators who had to fill it out. One of the ironies of the project was that, after agreeing that students should have this kind of information, several of the participating institutions experienced considerable strain in collecting and presenting such information about their own aid programs.

It is encouraging that the state of Oregon plans to incorporate the essence of the model statement in its computer-assisted Career Information System. Using information provided voluntarily by post-secondary institutions in the state, the Career Information System will enable prospective students to obtain an estimate of the appropriate student expense budget and the average student aid package (including Basic Grant, state grant, other grant, loan, and work awards) which students of their status (dependent or independent) and family income level received at a given institution in the preceding year. These data will be grouped in such a way as to show clearly the "net cost" to the student and his/her family; that is, the amount that must be provided from noninstitutional and nonaid resources in order to pay for the education sought. This specific cost and aid information will be supplemented by details of the application process, deadlines, required forms, and so forth.

The system developed in Oregon is currently being exported to six other states, under funding from the Department of Labor. Another ten states are actively considering implementation of the Oregon system. Although existing data may not be complete or accurate enough to permit these other states to include the detailed cost and aid information segment initially, the Oregon model will serve to point the way. The College Board is now working to develop the system for collecting and analyzing data that will be needed to facilitate state-wide implementation of the recommendations of our project.

While believing that institutions have the primary responsibility for providing complete and accurate information, our project committee was firm in the conviction that communication should be a partnership activity. As a first step in actualizing that partnership, we proposed a national campaign to increase public awareness of the true costs of postsecondary education and of the aid alternatives available. Financial support and direction for this campaign would come from the federal government, but other participants would include the national need analysis services, postsecondary institutions, secondary schools, community information and counseling services, benefit programs like Social Security and Veterans Administration, public and private media, students, and parents. The purposes of the campaign would be to promote financial aid as the means of access and choice in postsecondary education, to increase the prospective student's awareness of the true net costs of postsecondary education, and to create consumer demand for (and expectation of receiving) better information.

Such a campaign could be carried out for an estimated .01 percent of the 1978 allocation for the federal Basic Grant program. That seems a small contribution to make toward the development of consumer awareness. As prices continue to rise, a college education may become the biggest investment many families make. Without fair, complete, and accurate information on the costs of that education and on the aid available, they cannot make informed decisions about that investment. Without such information, programs that simply provide aid will be less than successful. Without institutional commitment to providing that information, all the mandatory disclosure language written by the Congress will fail. The *perceived* financial burden of a postsecondary education (whatever the validity of that perception) will continue to discourage prospective students and thus to frustrate national efforts to achieve equality of access and choice. Some commentators object to the use of the term *consumerism* to describe the changing relationship between students and institutions on the grounds that it reduces education to the level of a refrigerator or a box of cereal being purchased by some consumer. But unless prospective students and their families receive at least as much relevant information as other consumers do, more mandatory disclosure provisions will appear in future legislation. This is an outcome that no educator wants to see. If institutions will characterize their new relationship with students by fair, honest, accurate, and complete reporting of financial information, more Javits language will not be necessary. It is up to the institutions to get the word out.

Tidying Up the Policy Space

D. BRUCE JOHNSTONE

A POPULAR LATE-NIGHT TV PROGRAM features a routine in which Ed McMahon reads a seemingly meaningless word or phrase, whereupon Johnny Carson responds with a question that turns Ed's contribution into an uproariously funny answer. Comedy happens not to be my strong suit, and I suspect that financial aid and the costs of college are not very good material anyway. But I have always enjoyed figuring out a question when already supplied with the answer, an exercise that is often a good deal more challenging than the conventional process of beginning with the question.

For example, let us take the title of this panel, *The Financial Burden of a College Education,* as an answer and see what questions come to mind. How about, What is it that we simply cannot keep passing on to the student in the form of more debt? Or, What is it that we cannot expect the taxpayer to bear any more of, particularly when he is already groaning under the twin burdens of taxation and inflation—and besides, the kids can't find jobs anyway? Or, What is it that continues to deny to the poor the same chances for personal fulfillment and occupational mobility that are enjoyed by the well-to-do? Or, What is it that is heaviest for students from middle-class families who don't have grants like the lucky poor or lots of money like the even luckier rich? Or, What is it that just can't keep increasing? Or, What is it that is bound to keep increasing, as college costs continue to rise faster than nontuition sources of revenue? Or, What is it that over eleven million students—with help from parents, spouses, work, scholarships, and loans—are managing somehow to cope with?

To each of these questions, "the financial burden of a college education" is a suitable answer. Yet the juxtaposition of these seven questions—none in itself patently foolish, yet contradictory and shallow when taken together—reveals something about the current state of policy discussion about the costs of college.

Something is obviously wrong when expenses this year may be more than $7,000 for a private college freshman and as high as $9,000 for a beginning medical student. These costs have risen between 7 and 8 percent in each of the past six years, a rate of increase which is only a shade above that in the public sector. If the current rate of increase continues, this year's entering freshman at a private college will have spent as much as $50,000 by the time he or she finishes college in the spring of 1983.

But the old "compound-growth-rate" trick is a cheap scare, a close cousin to the rhetorical-points-disguised-as-questions which began this paper. What is needed in a discussion of the financial burden of college is less scare and rhetoric and more attention to three questions. First, what are the real problems of the high and rising costs of college? Second, what are the givens and the constraints that limit our responses to these problems? And third, what, then, are the issues and alternatives that ought to be receiving our analytical and deliberative energies?

The answers to these questions form what I call the *policy space* around college costs. This three-dimensional, nonlinear imagery of space is deliberate. Policy-makers are surrounded by problems, alternatives, and consequences. They become preoccupied with those that are nearest; that is, the most visible or vocal problems, the most familiar or comprehensible "solutions." Ideally, the policy space should embrace most closely those issues that are both socially important and amenable to policy. When that which is closest is trivial or contradictory or when it cannot be affected by policy anyway, the result is inaction, wrong action, or frustration.

Currently, the policy space surrounding the financial burden of higher education is chaotic, cluttered with nonissues, with alternatives that no policy-maker is free to choose, and with "solutions" that create greater problems than those they were devised to solve. I want to tidy up the policy space just a little by suggesting some fundamental problems, some limits to policy, and some major issues that should occupy the attention of those constructively concerned with the high and rising costs of college.

The problem of college expenses

The mere demonstration that college is, or can be, expensive or "a burden," or even that some people cannot or will not go to college or to a particular college because of the expense, is not sufficient to establish "a problem." Homes, suede suits, steak dinners, and appendectomies are also expensive. Anything expensive can be called a burden to those who have to pay for it if they do not have much money or if there are a lot of things they would much rather have than this particular expensive thing.

The high and rising expense of college unquestionably seems like a problem: to those who are paying it, to those who feel they cannot pay for it, and to those institutions for which either the present high prices or the possible remedies to them are a threat. But which of these problems properly belong in our policy space? I suggest three criteria for judging the problems most worthy of our attention: (1) the fundamental invidiousness of the problem; (2) the degree to which it is in fact present, and (3) the causal link between the problem and the high and rising expense of college.

By these criteria, the denial of equal opportunity for fulfilling individual academic potential remains the principal problem connected with the financial burden of a college education. It is the most invidious of the possible consequences of the financial burden. It is clearly a condition that actually exists. And the causal link between costs, aid, and equalization of opportunity is a sure one. This problem, then, is the most prominent in our policy space.

By contrast, the problem of financial burden upon students already attending college or upon their parents is not sufficiently damaging or invidious or amenable to policy alteration to deserve much attention in the policy space. True, it is a highly visible irritant, and it is directly linked to tuition and financial aid, but it does not change college-going behavior or otherwise made a difference either to the student or to society. However, the growing momentum behind tax credits for educational expenses suggests that others do not share this judgment.

Another potential problem is the distortion of choice between schools or programs that may be forced upon some students not merely by high and rising costs, but by price disparities between the public and independent sectors, between high- and low-tuition schools, and between commuting and resident opportunities. This problem is worthy of atttention to the degree that it denies needy students basic life and career choices; it is less, if at all, worthy to the degree that some students simply get the chance to consume a more or less expensive education than others. Admittedly, the line is a fine one. Similarly, the distortion of choice is an important social problem to the degree that precious academic resources are being wasted in private institutions which, because of price competition from the public sector, are no longer able to attract enough students to fully use their faculties. But this seems not to be the case. Although the independent sector has seen little growth, particularly in comparison with the public sector, it is not conspicuous in its wastage, nor is the disparity between public and private tuitions the sole factor behind the shaky prospects of the independent sector. The disparity of financial burdens between the public and private sectors, then, creates some problems worthy of our policy space. But the relationships are complex, and the problems neither so serious in themselves nor so amenable to policy solutions as the problem of unequal opportunity.

Limits of the policy space

As both makers and analysts of policy discover early—and to their dismay—the policy space around most issues is actually very narrow; that is, many of the key components are quite beyond the reach of policy. The cost of college to the student/family unit is constrained in at least five ways, which are summarized below in approximate order of their immutability.

First, the underlying costs (as distinct from the prices) of higher education will continue to rise at a rate close to that of before-tax wages and salaries. Any productivity gains—and few if any dramatic gains are likely—will be absorbed by deferred salary and maintenance needs, which have lagged far behind in recent years.

Second, an increasing proportion of students will be older, part time, and clearly independent of parental support. Nearly half of the nation's college students are over twenty-one, one-tenth are over thirty-five. For most of this group, the concept of need based upon parents' income—a concept that has formed the cornerstone of our financial aid system—is utterly inadequate. Rather than parental support, they must rely on their own present and future earnings, and on support from spouse or from the general taxpayer.

A third constraint is that parents through the upper-middle-income range are contributing about as great a proportion of their income and assets as they can or will, at least toward private education. According to standard need analysis procedures, a family of four with one child in college and an adjusted gross income of $16,000 should contribute more than $1,000 to the support of that student; an adjusted gross income of $30,000 would be "taxed" for about $4,750. Since these amounts are higher than normal current savings for such families, they have two alternatives: either they must cut back greatly on current consumption, borrow, or liquidate assets; or they must reduce the burden by choosing a lower-priced education for their child.

Fourth, because of slow growth in the economy plus the pressure of other urgent social needs plus the likelihood of a continuing tight job market for many college graduates, state government will be hard-pressed just to keep up with their share of the rising costs of college education—much less be able to assume a portion of the share now being borne by students or parents.

Finally, federal outlays for higher education, which more than doubled between 1972 and 1976, are inextricably bound up in social security and veterans benefits, in Basic Opportunity Grants, and in the growing costs of the federal loan programs. As the college population stabilizes, as the Basic Grants program matures, and as veterans aid winds down, the federal programs may be able to keep up more readily with increasing costs and prices rather than having continually to accommodate new entrants into the system. For example, large appropriations for aid programs would probably result in (a) elevation of the ceiling on Basic Grants, removal of the half-cost limitation, and full funding of the program; (b) an increase in funds for the Supplemental Equal Opportunity Grant program, indirectly targeted on the private sector; and (c) the reemergence of aid for graduate and advanced professional school students, selected according to need, ability, field of study, or a combination of these three. Thus, any increase in direct federal aid funds will go, first, toward keeping up the federal share of rising costs for current federal aid recipients; second, toward making up some of the shortfalls left by the failure of state or institutional aid to increase with inflation; and third, toward expanding opportunities to those not yet reached. Only fourth—if a massive program of tax relief for middle-income families in the form of cost-of-education tax credits finally gets past the House after a decade of support in the Senate—will large amounts of federal funds go toward lessening the real burden faced by the average student and his or her family. Such a tax credit, if not absorbed by an increase in the expected parental contribution, would give a small measure of relief to families—at least to those lucky enough both to pay federal income taxes and to have children in college. Therefore, federal aid may in the future relieve many students and parents a little and a few students and parents a lot; but a widespread and significant lessening of the financial burden of higher education is not likely to come from the federal government.

Principal issues

Given the problems and limits summarized above, a few major issues must occupy most of the policy space surrounding the financial burden of college. I suggest five.

To what extent should we attempt to induce further enrollments by lowering the cost of college? There are—and, in the absence of universal compulsory higher education, will continue to be—many young people who do not attend college. Some lack even the rudimentary skills for college; others lack the interest; others, both. Expressed positively, many of them undoubtedly prefer the income and life style of the nonacademic world to the sacrifices and demands of college. Were the nonattenders not disproportionately from low-income and minority families, we might conclude that the possibility (with Basic Grants and loans) of anyone's going to (some) college, coupled with the fact that over eleven million people are currently enrolled, suggests that we do not need to induce many more into the system. But patterns of socioeconomic status, race, location, and sex do exist, and we cannot rest so content. At the same time, it is not at all clear how far a more equalitarian participation in higher education should or can be achieved by financial inducements.

To what degree should the higher tuitions charged by independent colleges be taken into account in determining the amounts of state and federal grants to which students are entitled? As enrollments have shifted to the public sector, and as a period of almost certain decline in the student population approaches, proponents of a strong independent sector seek to protect their enrollments and their income by reducing the price disparity between the two sectors. The alternative of raising public tuitions to help the private sector has never had a serious place in the policy space. But financial aid from state or federal sources can lessen the price disparity if a student can get a higher award by electing a high-priced private college than by electing a lower-priced public one. This underlying issue will continue to be reflected in debates over the relative funding of the Supplemental Equal Opportunity Grant program, the half-cost limitation on Basic Opportunity Grants, and possible further changes in the BEOG formula.

To what degree should criteria other than financial need enter into the determination of financial assistance? Financial assistance is a potentially powerful lever for bringing about changes in the fortunes of certain schools, of certain programs within schools, and of certain kinds of students. This is not to say that grants given on the basis of need alone are necessarily neutral. They probably tend, among other things, to distribute students among more institutions and to level out institutional differences in academic quality. But any other criterion— for example, academic promise, presumed quality of a particular school or program, presumed national need for certain kinds of trained manpower—involves the active and continuing judgments of fallible men and women. And any form of financial assistance that ignores need altogether may deprive some students of the resources they must have to go to college at all.

To what degree should the present expected parental contributions be reduced, and to whom should that responsibility be shifted? Because parents today contribute directly some $4 billion toward the college expenses of their children, and because no one has suggested that their burden be lessened by denying educational opportunities to their children, the two parts of this issue must be addressed together. The only parties in the policy space who might be given a portion of the responsibility now borne by parents are (1) their children through a replacement of some expected parental contribution with more student debt; (2) other, more affluent parents, through even higher tuitions for those who can afford to pay, with a portion of the additional revenues going toward the increased grants required by a reduction in the expected parental contributions; or (3) those taxpayers without children in college and consumers generally, through a tax credit to parents of college-going children, paid for by other federal taxes or by deficit-induced inflation.

There is nothing sacred about the present expectation of parental support. A perfectly equitable system of financing higher education could have been constructed giving no financial responsibility at all to parents. But the existing system draws $4 billion from parents who can pay, or at any rate who do pay. To forego a significant portion of those resources—even indirectly through a tax credit—will require a commensurate increase in other taxes or tuition at a time when these sources are hard-pressed to maintain their present shares. Such a shift would not significantly alter enrollment patterns, since the primary beneficiaries would be the parents of students already enrolled. And the shift of net income—from the general taxpayer and consumer to the taxpayer with heavy college expenses—is almost certain to be, on the average, a shift from the less well-off to the more well-off. Yet tax credits and other forms of income transfer to the middle and upper-middle class have enormous political appeal and so will remain an option in our policy space. My hope is that they will be associated with the proper issue and debated as much as possible on their real consequences.

To what extent can and should students be expected to go further into debt so as to lighten the financial load now borne by taxpayers and parents? In the 1976–77 academic year, some 866,000 students borrowed some $1.8 billion through the federally sponsored student loan programs. Students graduating from private colleges in 1981 may well have an average accumulated indebtedness of $5,000; many graduates of public institutions wil not lag far behind. And this indebtedness can easily triple or quadruple by the end of graduate school.

At this point, no one even seriously questions whether student debt can be frozen or rolled back, much less whether students sought to borrow at all. Within the policy space of college expenses, student debt can only rise. This is not to suggest for a moment that it should rise at a faster rate than all other sources of support. Indeed, it is of great concern that graduate and advanced professional school debt is increasing more sharply than any other source. But student borrowing—again, particularly at the graduate and advanced professional levels—may in the short run have considerably greater elasticity than either the parental contribution or the public purse. If so, expectations about "self-help" will increase, and the intergenerational shift of responsibility from today's parents to today's students may continue.

I have suggested five major issues connected with the financial burden of a college education. They are the issues that I believe belong within the policy space surrounding the high costs of college. Perhaps there are six or eight rather than five, and certainly they could be worded differently. My point is that the issues are not so very many, the alternatives are relatively few, and the consequences of most choices are apparent.

The financial burden of college is a problem. There is no yet-undiscovered "solution" that will ease the burden for some without shifting it to others. But there are some policies that are better than others. We have a better chance of choosing the better policies if we simplify and tidy up the policy space.

Addressing Costs and Questioning Benefits

BRUCE FULLER

FOR THE PROSPECTIVE STUDENT, the task of financing a college education remains difficult. Yet the objective is clear, and the resources are usually available. For the legislator attempting to help prospective students or collegiate institutions, higher education finance becomes a maze of conflicting objectives and competing constituencies, a world of formulae, acronyms, and printouts. Yet the decisions of state appropriation committee members clearly make a difference with respect to the financial burden that students and their families must bear. Three financing issues are of particular interest.

- What social values and priorities underlie various patterns of financing students and colleges?
- Should (and will) the states' share of support be increased?

• In what ways does questioning the benefits of higher education affect students' and government's perceptions of costs?

The first and second of these issues relate to the choices that colleges and legislatures must make in meeting higher education's costs. The third, and most intriguing, relates to increasing skepticism—on the part of students and of government officials—about the benefits of traditional colleges; this skepticism clearly affects the financing choices of families and legislators.

Social values and priorities

Institutional and legislative decisions about financing will depend on the way in which three questions—each of which embodies competing social values and priorities—are answered. First, should financial assistance be concentrated on the most needy or on the highest achievers? This is the clearest social-class issue facing higher education today. Great progress has been made in moving from merit-based to need-based student aid, but institutional support policies in many states remain regressive. Despite California's cultural plurality, its higher education system is close to the most stratified (innocently termed "differentiated") in the nation. The University of California— serving the brightest 12.5 percent of high school graduates, who are generally from the wealthiest families—receives the highest per-student subsidy from the state. The state's community colleges, serving students from the poorest background, spend far less per student.

Second, should public money be used to serve students or institutions? A large share of appropriated institutional support goes for administration, research, and faculty salary increases. Many legislators, impatient with bureaucracies, are choosing to increase direct aid to students rather than to increase institutional support; cash transfer programs seem more desirable to many of those concerned with higher education and other social areas.

Third, should a college opportunity be provided to the many, or should a choice of colleges be provided to a few? As enrollments level off and even decline, this question increasingly divides low-cost state institutions from high-cost private ones. Private colleges advocate larger student-aid grants to cover tuition increases, while public colleges favor expansion of the number of grants to serve additional students. If President Carter is serious about balancing the federal budget, fiscal pressures will accentuate these conflicting priorities. In California, the legislature and the governor have in recent years chosen to help additional students rather than to give larger grants to fewer students.

Viewed in the context of these three questions, the 1972 creation and continued expansion of the federal Basic Educational Opportunity Grant program can be seen as a culmination of radical shifts in federal financing policies: the Basic Grant program is intended to promote wider access through direct aid to the neediest students.

Providing low-income students access to postsecondary education has become a dominant federal goal. According to the Congressional Budget Office, 51 percent ($7.4 billion) of all fiscal year 1977 expenditures for postsecondary education went toward achieving equality of opportunity; slightly over 15 percent ($2.2 billion) went toward the goal of "easing the financial burden"; and the remaining 33 percent ($4.8 billion) was allocated to improving institutional capacities (e.g., support of research and of categorical programs).[1]

At the same time, some middle-income families are having difficulty financing a college education for their children, and political pressure to increase aid to middle-income students has been mounting, often with observable effects. For instance, in California, the median family income of state scholarship recipients jumped from $11,700 to $14,200 in just one year.

The financial problems of middle-income students cannot be denied, but they should not be exaggerated either. Student fees at public colleges have remained constant at 13 percent of middle-class family income since 1967.[2] Moreover, despite the growth in federal and state equal opportunity programs (EOP), middle-income students continue to enter college at more than twice the rate of low-income students.[3]

In addressing the rising costs of college attendance, government and institutional policy-makers must maintain and strengthen this nation's commitment to the poor. The first priority must be to refine the attack on barriers that still deter the most needy from entering

1. *Postsecondary Education: The Current Federal Role and Alternative Approaches* (Washington: Government Printing Office, 1977), p. xvii.

2. Ibid., p. 21.

3. Bureau of the Census, *School Enrollment—Social and Economic Characteristics of Students: October 1974*, P-20, No. 286 (Washington: Government Printing Office, 1975).

postsecondary education. Although better data are needed on how the federal Basic Grant and state student aid programs have affected the college-going decisions of low-income students, there is some evidence to suggest that financial need may soon be eliminated as a barrier to access. As early as 1972, national college-entry rates among high-achieving, low-income high school graduates were comparable to those for middle-income students.[4] In California, of the inner-city high school graduates eligible to enter a state college, a surprising 74 percent actually enroll in a four-year institution, and another 10 percent enter a community college. The problem is that three times as many high school graduates from high-income areas as from low-income areas are eligible to enter state institutions.[5] Even more appalling, many inner-city high schools have dropout rates as high as 40 percent. Clearly, high school achievement is related to family income. But more than just financial aid is needed if low-achieving, inner-city high school graduates are to be served.

This is not an argument against increases in student aid programs. My point is that further progress toward the goal of equal educational opportunity requires (1) greater efforts in the secondary schools to raise the achievement level—and thus increase the college-entry rate—of disadvantaged students and (2) additional resources for comprehensive EOP programs to increase the college persistence rate of disadvantaged students. Advocates of equal opportunity must shift their focus to nonfinancial services, including recruitment, tutoring, and counseling. For low-income high school students who are unaware of postsecondary opportunities and who lack both motivation and grades, college attendance is simply not a realistic choice, no matter how much financial aid is available. And for low-income students who do enroll in college, the financial aid that made possible their enrollment will be wasted if they soon drop out because of lack of supportive services.

Even as Congress has been expanding the Basic Grant program, many states have cut back on support for comprehensive educational opportunity programs that provide support services. As a result, many disadvantaged students find themselves enrolled in institutions that

4. *Postsecondary Education*, p. 13.

5. Assembly Subcommittee on Postsecondary Education, *Unequal Access to College: Postsecondary Opportunities and Choices of High School Graduates* (Sacramento: California Legislature, 1975).

cannot meet their needs. For example, only 12 percent of EOP students at the City University of New York complete the baccalaureate program within five years.[6] The cost implications of such a high attrition rate are enormous.

Only six states spend more than $2 million annually for EOP efforts. Since 1971–72, the state of New York has cut support of its educational opportunity program (the nation's largest) from $44 million to $39 million (an 11 percent decrease), whereas total state support for postsecondary education has climbed by over 50 percent.[7] Congressional action this year to increase funding for the Trio Programs—Upward Bound, Talent Search, and Special Services—from $70 million to $115 million is the one bright spot in an otherwise bleak picture.

Another step that would benefit not just the disadvantaged but all prospective students and their families is simplification of the vast and complicated student aid "system." Some progress in this direction is being made. For example, the Office of Education's recent decision to share financial information on applicants with private need-analysis services and state student-aid agencies will help to reduce the paperwork for applicants. California has moved to consolidate existing undergraduate aid programs and to implement a common application form.

The state's share

A recent report in the Carnegie Council series notes four remarkable financing shifts in higher education that have occurred since 1929–30:[8]

- The aggregate cost of higher education (including student subsistence costs but excluding foregone income) has increased fifteenfold; from $1.6 billion to $25 billion (in terms of 1967 constant dollars); the educational costs of institutions has increased twenty-three times over.

6. Assembly Subcommittee on Postsecondary Education, *Educational Opportunity Programs: National Views of State Issues* (Sacramento: California Legislature, 1977).

7. Ibid.

8. Carnegie Foundation for the Advancement of Teaching, *The States and Higher Education: A Proud Past and a Vital Future* (San Francisco: Jossey-Bass, 1976).

• Primary support of higher education has shifted from private to public sources. The private share (comprising current gifts and endowment income, and expenditures by students and their families) fell from 79 percent to 41 percent. Public support of student costs (through student aid programs) rose from 21 percent to 59 percent; public support of institutions rose from 42 percent to 68 percent.

• The federal share of support for higher education jumped from 9 percent to 45 percent.

• Taxpayers, not students and their families, have felt most of the brunt of these increases. The net cost borne by students and their families actually dropped by 9 percent, mostly because of state and federal student aid programs and other programs (e.g., Veterans Administration) that provide education benefits. Whereas per-capita real income tripled during the period, the tax burden per student to the state taxpayer more than tripled.

It is unlikely that public support will continue to grow at this rate. Increasing federal support of low-income students may result in a greater degree of income transfer, but state support of higher education is leveling off and may actually decrease. Currently, two factors affect prospects for state financing of higher education: the mood of the taxpayer and the heavy competition for tax dollars.

First, the cost of all levels of government now accounts for 37 percent of the gross national product, compared with 12 percent in 1929. This growth has had some highly positive effects, such as reducing the proportion of the poverty-level population from 17 percent in 1965 to 12 percent a decade later.[9] Nonetheless, angered by the rising cost of all government services, many taxpayers are more interested in tax relief than in expansion of social programs. As a consequence, many nominally "liberal" Democrats are taking the politically safe course of fiscal conservatism. For example, while California's Governor Brown has worked successfully with the legislature to expand financial aid and support service for low-income students, he is just as tough on institutional budgets as Governor Reagan was.

Second, the competition for public money has intensified, especially among human development fields. Not only do advocates of other social programs such as child care and youth employment claim

9. "Big Government," *Newsweek*, December 15, 1975.

that their area has more urgent priority than higher education, but also they have recently become better organized at obtaining public funds, as is evidenced by the expansion of Trio Programs this year. Moreover, new education constituencies may be undermining traditional higher education interests. Thus, the emergence of teachers unions has stimulated considerable legislative activity in K-12 finance, diverting political energy and public dollars from higher education. Similarly, student lobbies—emphasizing that the interests of students do not always coincide with the interests of administrators—have challenged conventional allocation patterns, pushing for direct student aid and support for categorical programs rather than for general institutional aid.

Even in those cases where state appropriations for higher education have increased recently, the additional funds are often those requested not by the institutional leadership but by special interests, such as minority groups and students, and thus are earmarked for specific purposes such as EOP and instructional improvement. Further increases in state aid to institutions will probably do no more than cover faculty salary increases and other costs related to inflation. To attract additional state dollars, higher education may have to concentrate on developing categorical programs that address specific problems or serve particular constituencies.

Causes and consequences of skepticism

Growing skepticism about the benefits of higher education inevitably affects the spending decisions of prospective students and legislators. The value of a college education is being challenged from all sides. In purely economic terms, students enrolled in college lose $25 billion annually in foregone income.[10] As Richard Freeman has demonstrated, the economic return of a college degree (in terms of lifetime earnings) has declined.[11] The waste of human resources represented by unemployed and underemployed college graduates suggests that something is deeply wrong with our economy, our educational institutions, or both.

Moreover, the noneconomic benefits bestowed by higher education may be too narrow as society becomes more pluralistic. Daniel Yankelovich has documented substantial change in the life styles,

10. *The States and Higher Education.*
11. *The Overeducated American* (New York: Academic Press, 1976).

moral values, politics, and attitudes of young people both in and out of school.[12] But it is questionable whether higher education has evolved in such a way as to keep pace with these changes. Too often it seems to have remained beset by the "homogenization" identified in the First Newman Report.[13]

Traditional higher education's remoteness from the vital centers of our diverse culture became clearer to me after I read recent books by Charles Reich, Jerry Rubin, and Carl Rogers.[14] In the past, each of these writers was concerned with the external world: Reich examined broad cultural trends, Rubin urged mass political action, and Rogers looked at group relationships. Now all three have turned inward: Reich and Rubin explore their own personal growth and its connections with social change. Rogers argues that, as individuals move toward fuller personal development and greater self-determination, authoritarian institutions must evolve to allow for shared decision making and a greater plurality of values.

Reich, Rubin, and Rogers are connecting with many people in our culture who are exploring themselves, trying out new relationships, and experimenting with various life styles. Though it is a commonplace to claim that today's young are apathetic and socially irresponsible, the vigor with which they pursue self-fulfillment and personal freedom gives the lie to this charge. The human potential movement will undoubtedly help to shape our social and political future.

Yet academic institutions have remained largely untouched by and unresponsive to this movement. They continue to emphasize the primacy of rational empiricism, the fragmentation of knowledge into "disciplines," and the transmittal of knowledge by "experts" to a passive audience. Such an approach is distant from immediate and pressing human questions. For example, to what extent does conventional higher education help individuals and society to cope with the problems of marriage, energy consumption, and employment? The

12. *The New Morality: A Profile of American Youth in the 70's* (New York: McGraw-Hill, 1974).

13. *Report on Higher Education* (Washington: Government Printing Office, 1971.

14. Reich, *The Sorcerer of Bolinas Reef* (New York: Random, 1976); Rubin, *Growing Up at 37* (New York: M. Evans, 1976); Rogers, *On Personal Power* (New York: Delacorte, 1977).

very success of mass education reveals the limited utility of purely cognitive learning. The critical choices that people make involve human values and life styles.

All this is not intended to deny the contributions of higher education. Nor am I saying that public dollars should be reallocated to the human potential movement or marijuana decriminalization efforts. My point is simply that prospective and current students may perceive the costs of a college education as excessive in light of its (presumed) diminishing returns.

The choices of state policy-makers are similarly constrained by skepticism. This year during legislative budget hearings, a reluctant University of California was urged to improve undergraduate teaching, to assess the impact of agricultural mechanization research on rural employment, to shift toward training more primary-care physicians, to conduct research on low-energy technology, and to refrain from tightening admissions requirements and thus reducing minority enrollments. All these issues were raised by external constituencies; the university had not addressed them prior to the legislative discussions. Such indifference to fundamental human and social problems cannot but provoke skepticism among legislators. Though such skepticism can be ignored in the short run, in the long run it leads to a diffusion of political support that will prove costly to the university and to all Californians.

Many administrators and faculty members dismiss the criticisms of students and external groups as intrusive and unsophisticated. So resentful are they of questioning by outsiders that they simply ignore the specific issues raised. But enrollment declines and the steady state will soon make it impossible for them to maintain this defensive position. As improvement rather than expansion of social programs is increasingly emphasized and as legislative oversight activity becomes more intense, academic institutions will simply have to accept and respond to thoughtful and constructive criticism from students and external groups.

It is to be hoped that academic leaders can become more introspective, more inclined to question the benefits of higher education as measured against pluralistic student and community needs. Higher education's predominant values are still appropriate, but a broader vision of academic freedom and excellence is necessary to accommodate diverse, often competing, needs: Research *and* undergraduate teaching must be rewarded; academic knowledge *and* human relationships must be highly valued; the talents of disadvantaged students *and* high achievers must be developed.

To the extent that prospective students and legislators perceive positive benefits from higher education, its costs will seem small. Unless higher education responds to diverse student and community needs, however, its benefits will seem narrow and its costs will seem too high.

Institutional Liabilities

MICHAEL A. LIETHEN

THE FOCUS OF STUDENT LITIGATION in education has changed. The great explosion of litigation in the 1960s was touched off by the civil rights movement and the Vietnam war, both of which raised fundamental moral questions for many students. Academic institutions, as representatives of the establishment, became the object of confrontations which were intended to bring those issues to the public consciousness. When colleges and universities sought to regulate student protest, the legal battle was joined. Reflecting the circumstances of its origin, this early litigation usually centered on the constitutional adequacy of student disciplinary proceedings, the limits of the institution's authority to regulate speech, and (to a much lesser extent) the institution's right to regulate other areas of student life, such as dress and parietal rules.

As the times have changed, so has the thrust of legal challenges to colleges and universities. Growing concern over the quality and safety of products has led to the development of a body of law creating liability for defective and dangerous products. Nor have providers of services been immune, as is evidenced by the medical malpractice crisis. And the lawyers themselves, who made all this possible, are themselves becoming more frequent targets of similar litigation. Consumerism has come to the campus because it has come to the rest of the economy. Another motive force behind student consumerism is the tight job market for college graduates. Students concerned about their employment potential are looking more closely at the quality of the education they receive. When an institution's performance does not meet the expectations of these newly critical education consumers, they may turn to the courts for redress.

Institutional officers should therefore prepare for closer judicial scrutiny of the educational process. During the 1960s, social trends propelled colleges and universities into situations which they did not an-

43

ticipate and for which they were unprepared, and the resultant judicial intervention caused some dislocation. To avoid judicial intervention arising from this new consumer awareness, institutions would be wise to spend resources in self-evaluation aimed at anticipating legal entanglements and taking preventive measures now. In particular, administrators should understand the potentials for legal liability. In this paper, I will cover three theories of liability: torts, contracts, and constitutional law.[1]

Much of the litigation against colleges and universities is founded upon constitutional theory, which is limited in application to public institutions because the Fourteenth Amendment concepts of due process and equal protection apply only to "state action." Liability based upon the law of contract or the law of torts is not similarly restricted; indeed, because of sovereign immunity, public institutions may frequently be immune to contract or tort litigation.

Torts is that body of law which provides redress for wrongful injury, physical or emotional, done to one person by another; it includes the law of negligence, intentional torts, and misrepresentation (negligent or intentional).

Negligence

The law of negligence has proved to be flexible, allowing the courts to fashion remedies for wrongs in novel situations, as when the charge is that classroom instruction is of poor quality because of teacher incompetence or negligence or because the institution has not devoted sufficient resources to the educational program. To prove a case based on negligence, the plaintiff must prove (1) that the defendant has a legal duty to conform to a standard of conduct established by law for the protection of the plaintiff; (2) that the defendant has failed to conform to that standard of conduct; (3) that such failure is a legal cause of the harm suffered by the plaintiff; and (4) that the plaintiff has in fact suffered harm legally compensable by damages.[2]

In cases involving the quality of classroom instruction, the relief sought might include removal of an incompetent teacher from the classroom (with negligence constituting just cause for dismissal), provision of remedial instruction or of payments to the plaintiff so that the stu-

---

1. This discussion of tort and contract theories is highly simplified. A thorough discussion of these theories can be found in "Educational Malpractice," *University of Pennsylvania Law Review*, 1976, p. 755.

2. Restatement (second) of Torts, Section 328A (1965).

dent can obtain the instruction elsewhere, or monetary compensation for such injury as total provable reduction in future income because of the limited employment potential resulting from inadequate education. Obstacles to a negligence action include theories of governmental or charitable immunity, the possibility that the student rather than the teacher is at fault for the educational deficiency, and the difficulty of proving that the teacher has not exercised the degree of skill or training ordinarily possessed by members of the profession in the community or other similar communities.

The legal element of "duty" is especially troublesome; it is legal shorthand for "the sum total of those considerations of policy which lead the law to say that the particular plaintiff is entitled to protection."[3] The complaining student must therefore overcome social policy considerations suggesting that a school should not be held liable in tort for educational malpractice because a substantial money judgment for the plaintiff will only diminish the funds available for the education of others, will discourage useful and necessary educational experimentation, or will discourage talented people from entering the teaching profession. In one case recently brought against the San Francisco Unified School District, the parents of a high school graduate alleged that the school system negligently failed to provide adequate instruction, guidance, and counseling in basic academic skills such as reading and writing because it failed to recognize the student's reading disabilities, allowed him to pass from one grade to another without the skills necessary to succeed in subsequent grades, assigned him to classes taught by unqualified instructors, and permitted him to graduate even though he could not read above the eighth-grade level.[4] They sought damages for their son's impaired earning capacity and for his inability to gain meaningful employment. The court concluded, however, that public-policy considerations precluded a finding that the school system owed a legally recognized duty of care to the plaintiff.

Public policy can and does change; it may even vary from one community to another. Moreover, a particular court's view of that policy as applied to particular circumstances may lead to a finding of liability; for instance, when a situation is obviously outrageous or when

3. W. Prosser, *Handbook of the Law of Torts* (4th Ed., 1971) section 53, at 325–26.

4. Peter W. v. San Francisco Unified School District, 60 Cal. App. 3d, 814, 131 Cal. Rptr. 854 (1976).

the educational deficiency is beyond doubt (as when a specific statute or administrative regulation is unquestionably breached).

This theory may be summarized as intent (not necessarily to do harm) that "invades the interests of another in a way that the law will not sanction."[5] Examples are a faculty member who deliberately fails to teach the subject matter of a particular course as outlined in the school catalog or a teacher who deliberately humiliates a student in front of the class.

The elements of negligent or intentional misrepresentation are (1) false representation, (2) knowledge that the representation is false or based on insufficient information, (3) intention to induce the plaintiff to act in reliance on the misrepresentation, (4) justifiable reliance on the misrepresentation by the plaintiff, and (5) damage resulting from that reliance.

In 1959, Columbia University brought suit against a former student to recover on two loans. The student countercharged that the university was guilty of misrepresentation in that it had indicated that it would teach wisdom, truth, character, enlightenment, understanding, justice, liberty, honesty, and so forth.[6] Though this charge verged on the ridiculous (and, indeed, the student lost), some situations involve the serious possibility of institutional liability: as when a student is given a high grade in a first-semester language course and, upon enrolling in the second-semester course, discovers that she has not been taught the skills fundamental to satisfactory performance, or when a student is induced to enroll in a particular institution by catalog or bulletin listings of the courses available in a particular major only to discover that many of these courses are no longer offered and will not be offered in the foreseeable future.

Law of contracts

The second theory under which a college or university may incur liability is that of contract. Generally, an institution may be said to agree to provide nonnegligent instruction under certain conditions, in return for the student's agreement to pay tuition and fees and to abide by the institution's policies. Contract law has some advantages over

5. Prosser, supra, section 12, p. 31.
6. Trustees of Columbia University v. Jacobsen, 148 A.2d 63, 53 N.J. Super. 574 (App. Div.), aff'd., 31 N.J. 221, 156 A.2d 251 (1959).

tort law: It avoids the defense of governmental immunity, and the courts may find it a more acceptable theory on which to allow recovery. A disadvantage of contract law is that it allows a narrower range of damages to be recovered, those which may have been tacitly agreed upon by the parties.

The courts have construed official institutional publications describing policies, procedures, and offerings as evidence of the terms of the general bargain reached by the student and the college. In *Steinberg v. Chicago Medical School,* the institution was held to the stated terms of an informational brochure. Upon being turned down by the medical school, Steinberg alleged that the brochure constituted an invitation to make an offer, that his application and remittance of an application fee constituted an offer, and that the school's acceptance of both applications and fee created a contract. He further alleged that the school's admissions decisions were based upon considerations other than the criteria stated in the brochure: namely, the applicant's family relationship to faculty and trustees, and his ability to pledge large sums of money to the school. The court found that a valid cause of action had been stated.[7]

Several students brought suit against George Washington University, claiming breach of contract when medical school tuition increased substantially more than had been projected in the school's bulletin. While accepting the proposition that the provisions of an institutional bulletin become part of a contract, the court held that a determination of contractual obligation depended upon the general principles of contract construction; in this instance, what a reasonable person would expect. The court concluded that the projected tuition levels in question were not definite enough to make reasonably certain the promises of performance to be rendered.[8]

In contrast, the court found in favor of a student who sought a partial tuition refund from New York University for classes that had been cancelled for the remainder of the semester as a result of events during May 1970. Even though the university's bulletin provided that programs were subject to change without notice, the court concluded that the institution's contractual obligation to provide an education had been breached since the cancellation of classes could not reasonably

7. 41 Ill. App. 3d 804 (1976).

8. Basch v. George Washington University, 370 A.2d 1364 (D.C. Ct. App. 1977).

have been contemplated to be within the mutual agreements made under the contract.[9]

If an institution's written statements are not fair representations, the institution may be liable on the contractual theory of "promissory estoppel"; that is, the institution's representations are made binding by the student's detrimental reliance on them. Academic institutions would be well advised, then, to consider carefully whether they want to be held to the expectations that their bulletins, catalogs, and other publications can reasonably be said to create in prospective students. As enrollments decline and as institutions compete more fiercely for students, comparisons among institutions will come to play a greater role in the prospective student's college decisions, and a student who foregoes the opportunity to attend one institution because of another institution's representations about its programs may have a cause for action against the latter if those representations are false or misleading.

The terms of the contract are not immutable. In a 1969 breach-of-contract suit against Vassar College for liberalizing its parietal rules and allowing unlimited visiting hours by men, the court held that the college had no legal obligation not to change its rules and that, in the absence of a showing of abuse of discretion, the courts could not intervene.[10] A more recent case tested whether Georgia State University could change its graduation requirements by imposing a comprehensive examination where none had previously been required; finding that the new requirement was reasonable and that the student had received timely notice of the change, the court concluded that "the claim of a binding, absolute unchangeable contract is particularly anomalous in the context of training professional teachers" at the postgraduate level.[11] Another case involved a former Howard University medical student who had failed a first-year course and had not removed the deficiency in accordance with a university policy stating that such a student could either be dropped or allowed to continue and, if allowed to continue, could be required to audit any course. The student brought suit against the university, contending that it could not impose conditions that were not explicitly stated in its policy; since the only explicit provision concerned auditing, the university

9. Paynter v. New York University, 314 N.Y.S.2d 676, 64 Misc.2d 226 (1970).

10. Jones v. Vassar College, 299 N.Y.S.2d 283, 59 Misc.2d 296 (1969).

11. Mahavongsanan v. Hall, 401 F.Supp. 381, aff'd. 529 F.2d 448 (5th Cir. 1976).

had breached its contract by requiring him to retake and pass courses that he had already passed. The court held that such a narrow construction of the contract was unreasonable because it would hamper the institution's efforts to assist marginal students. The student, unable to show that the institution had otherwise acted unreasonably, lost his case.[12]

All these cases concern the explicit policies of institutions. In two very recent cases, contract law was applied to the quality of educational offerings. Ilene Ianniello alleged that the University of Bridgeport had breached its contract with her because a required course did not comply substantially with the bulletin course description; there were no tests, no critiques of her work, and little class discussion; the university failed to supervise the teaching of the course; and she received no benefit from it. She and a classmate, both of whom had failed to obtain teaching jobs, testified. The instructor's testimony on the content and objectives of the course was substantiated by six other class members, all of whom had obtained teaching jobs. Reasoning that the university and its faculty were best qualified to judge the content and quality of the course and that Ianniello could not set herself up as an expert on how the course should be taught, the court did not allow the case to go to the jury. At issue was the sufficiency of the evidence; the plaintiff had not met her burden of proof. The case did not establish that the courts cannot review the adequacy of a course, but only that, in the absence of expert testimony to support the allegations, the evidence was not sufficient to prove that the university had abused the discretion afforded it under the contract.[13]

The second case of this type had a different outcome. Eight former doctoral students were awarded more than $30,000 in damages for breach of contract by Vanderbilt University's Graduate School of Management. Though the case will almost certainly be appealed, the decision is instructive since it demonstrates that, given a proper fact situation, courts will review the adequacy of academic offerings. In this instance, the highly unstructured and innovative doctoral program, whose faculty came from diverse backgrounds, had encountered serious problems (especially tensions among faculty members) almost from its inception. A crash review of the program in April 1975 brought

12. Giles v. Howard University, 428 F.Supp. 603 (1977).
13. Ianniello v. University of Bridgeport, No. 100009 (Ct. Common Pleas, Fairfield County, Conn., 1977).

about the first real consensus among the faculty about what the nature of the program should be and resulted in substantial changes, including new academic requirements and examinations for testing student competency, which had not been contemplated in the 1973 guidelines under which the plaintiffs entered the program. They contended that these changes constituted a breach of contract, but the court disagreed, acknowledging the wide latitude that the courts have allowed educators. Instead, the court found that the 1975 changes indicated that no real doctoral program had existed previously, that the program to which the university had probably devoted inadequate resources had rapidly disintegrated in 1974–75, that the university had failed to act to reverse this degenerative process, and that it was the "total collapse" of the program which constituted the breach of contract.[14]

Constitutional law

A long line of cases has held that the courts will not review academic judgments unless they are arbitrary and capricious.[15] But the prevailing view, starting with the famous Dixon cases in 1961, is that constitutional due process decisions regulating student disciplinary proceedings fall into another category.[16] A recent case, now on appeal to the U. S. Supreme Court, is therefore of special interest.

A University of Missouri medical student was dismissed without a hearing on the grounds that, though her academic performance had been exceptional, her performance in the clinical portion of the program was inadequate. The court held that the dismissal stigmatized her in such a way as to make it impossible for her to continue her medical education and that it damaged her chances of employment in a medically related field. Thus, she was entitled to a hearing before the committees and the dean that had made the decision, at which she would have an opportunity to rebut the evidence leading to her dismissal and would be accorded all other rights of procedural due process.[17]

14. Lowenthal v. Vanderbilt University, No. A-8525 (Chancery Court, Davidson County) (August 15, 1977).

15. See, for example, Connelly v. University of Vermont, 244 F.Supp. 156 (D. Vt. 1765); Edde v. Columbia University, 8 Misc.2d 795, 168 N.Y.S.2d 643 (1957); Militana v. University of Miami, 236 So.2d 470 (Fla. App. 1970).

16. Dixon v. Alabama State Board of Education, 294 F.2d 150 (5th Cir. 1961), cert. denied, 368 U.S. 930, 82 S. Ct. 368, 7 L. Ed.2d 193.

17. Horowitz v. Board of Curators of the University of Missouri, 538 F.2d 1317, rehearing denied, 542 F. 2d 1335 (8th Cir. 1976).

Since the dismissal decision involved subjective judgments about such matters as the student's ability to cope maturely with criticism and her patient and peer relations—judgments on which the committee members themselves were divided—the issue is a difficult one. On one hand, such interpersonal factors may be regarded as relevant to the academic evaluation of a professional student; on the other hand, these evaluations may disguise arbitrary personal prejudices on the part of the evaluators. Thus, the case would seem to occupy a gray area between questions of academic evaluation and of student conduct, the latter being an area in which the courts are accustomed to applying due process considerations. Nevertheless, since the student was dismissed not for misconduct but for inadequacy of performance in an academic program, an affirmance by the Supreme Court should lead to serious reflection about the standards and procedures used for making academic judgments. While the courts will probably continue to give educators broad discretion in making judgments of academic quality, they may also be saying that the institution's procedures for making such judgments should be fair, that the judgments should be based on explicit and tenable criteria, and that the student-consumer should be able to confront the evaluators and question their conclusions about his or her overall performance in an academic program.

At the risk of oversimplifying complex legal theories of education consumerism, it is reasonable to say that academic institutions can probably avoid most situations involving legal liability if they engage in continuing self-evaluation, with a commitment to identifying and correcting those policies and practices which could mislead or misrepresent or which do not meet minimal standards of educational excellence. Elaine El-Khawas' *New Expectations for Fair Practice: Suggestions for Institutional Review* should provide an excellent starting point for institutions undertaking such self-evaluation.[18] Whatever the difficulties involved, such a process is necessary not so much because it can prevent the possibility of litigation but because it is sound educational practice.

18. Washington: American Council on Education, 1976.

A Student's View of Consumerism in Postsecondary Education

JOEL PACKER

IN DAYS PAST, when a buyer dealt face-to-face with neighborhood merchants, the concept of *caveat emptor*—"let the buyer beware"—may have been sufficient. In these days, when the average consumer is dealing with enormous and impersonal organizations that control and sell goods and services, that warning is no longer enough to protect against gross abuse and exploitation.

Individual students are at a distinct disadvantage in trying to deal with the vast postsecondary education community. James Coleman has remarked on what he calls the "asymmetry" in size and resources between the applicant and the institution: The institution can get a wealth of specific information on the prospective student, from high school transcripts, application forms, letters of evaluation, and reports from the national testing agencies and need analysis services, whereas the student must make important life choices on the basis of whatever information the institution sees fit to provide, plus hearsay and impressions gathered at random from friends and alumni.[1] But many students are no longer willing to tolerate the inequities of this situation.

In this paper, I will look at the modern consumer movement and at some of the factors that account for its spread to the campus, at the kinds of abuses that may occur in postsecondary education, and at steps that students themselves have been taking to correct these abuses. Finally, I will make recommendations for further steps to be taken by government agencies and by institutions.

The modern consumer movement is an offshoot of a more general concern for citizen participation in decision making that burgeoned in the 1960s. President Kennedy sparked this movement in his 1962 message to Congress, with its proclamation of consumer rights. Several members of Congress also gave impetus to the movement. As chairman of the antitrust and monopoly subcommittee of the Senate Judiciary Committee, Senator Estes Kefauver conducted investigations into

1. "The Principle of Symmetry in College Choice," *Report of the Commission on Tests* (New York: College Entrance Examination Board, 1970), pp. 19–21.

administratively set prices and into the drug industry. Senator Paul Douglas of Illinois introduced truth-in-lending legislation, which was finally enacted into law in 1968.

The person most responsible for making America aware of consumer rights and abuses is Ralph Nader. Pointing out the danger in automobiles and other products, Nader suggested a way to guard against such abuses—by organizing. He proposed that citizens form permanent organizations to protect their interests. Many such groups are in existence today, including Nader-inspired Public Interest Research Groups (PIRGs) on many college campuses. Nader has defined *consumerism* as "the relationship between the receiver of goods and services or their by-products and the perpetrator or seller of these goods and services, and that could include government as well as industry.[2] It certainly can and does include educational institutions.

The concept of students as consumers is relatively new, having come into vogue only within the last five years. Speaking in 1975, Robert Andringa, then Minority Counsel for the House Committee on Education and Labor, stated: "Consumer protection was definitely *not* an issue in the consideration of the 1972 Education Amendments, but it has already become a substantial issue in 1975 as Congress faces the extension of postsecondary education legislation for four more years from 1976 through 1980."[3]

Basically, the spread of consumerism to the college campus may be regarded as an inevitable and natural extension of the general consumer rights movement. Nonetheless, certain factors within postsecondary education have operated to accelerate the development of education consumerism. Nine such factors are discussed here.

Abuses by proprietary schools. The questionable advertising and recruiting techniques, the low quality of offerings, and the inequitable refund policies of some proprietary schools have raised public awareness about the possibility of consumer abuse in postsecondary education.

The rising default rates for Guaranteed Student Loans. An increasing number of students in the collegiate sector of postsecondary education as well as in the proprietary schools are defaulting on

2. "Consumerism and Higher Education," address delivered at the "Higher Education Listens" conference sponsored by the Eastern Regional Council of the American Association for Higher Education, December 4, 1971, in Baltimore.

3. Quoted by Layton Olson, "Consumer Protection in Postsecondary Education," *Options Handbook #1: Information Needed by the Student Consumer* (Washington: National Student Educational Fund, 1976).

federally guaranteed loans, thus bringing the federal government into the picture.

Declining college enrollments. As the traditional college-age population decreases (a trend that will continue through the 1980s), many postsecondary institutions find their enrollments leveling off and even declining. In the intensified competition for students, institutions frequently resort to aggressive recruitment techniques that may lead to abuses.

Changes in the age distribution of the college population. As a result of increased efforts to promote equal educational opportunity and to maintain enrollment levels in the face of declines in the eighteen-year-old population, the average age of college students has risen. Larger numbers of older students (in their twenties and above) are entering postsecondary education; their greater sophistication, maturity, and concern with their rights is a factor in heightened consumer awareness on the college campus.

A tighter job market. Economic conditions have made it increasingly difficult for college graduates to find jobs, let alone jobs in their field of training. As students start to question the value of a college degree, they are also taking a closer look at the quality of the education they receive.

Rising college costs. Students and their parents are being asked to bear an ever-heavier financial burden for a college education. Even at a public university, the student living away from home may pay as much as $3,000 per year. Today, a college education for their children is one of the largest investments many families make, second only to the purchase of a home. With any product or service, people become more wary as costs rise. They want not only to know, but also to have a voice in, how their money is being spent.

Growing "adultness" on the part of the college students. With the lowering of the age of majority, young people are now legally adults earlier; this change, together with the elimination of parietal rules at many institutions, has heightened the consciousness of even traditional-age college students, making them more aware of the rights guaranteed to them as adults and more concerned with being treated as adults in all respects.

Growing complexity of postsecondary education. The change in terminology—from "higher education" to "postsecondary education"—signals the increasing complexity of the system, which now includes vocational schools, proprietary schools, and other forms of job-training programs as well as the traditional collegiate sector. Confronted with more options, prospective students also need more and better information in order to make rational decisions. In addition, increased federal support for postsecondary education has created greater government demands for accountability.

Heavier reliance on private agencies to perform certain functions. More external agencies are becoming involved in postsecondary education. For instance, to be admitted to college, students must take standardized tests administered by outside agencies; to get financial aid, they must give information to the needs analysis services of private organizations. In addition, the government relies on private accrediting agencies to determine institutional eligibility for federal funds. As a result of the increasing presence of these external agencies on the postsecondary education scene, many students find themselves agreeing with the following sentiments expressed by Stephen Brill.

> If we regulate a local utility because people have no choice but to buy its product, it seems incredible to me that we don't regulate this consumer product [the College Board examinations] that has millions of involuntary customers and has far greater consequences than a telephone or electric bill.[4]

Perhaps all these factors can be summarized in a single question, What is the purpose of our postsecondary institutions? Many students are finding that their views on this matter differ from those of administrators. This disparity gives rise to another question: Who should determine that purpose? Students are asking for a greater voice in deciding the answer to that question.

The nature of consumer abuse

Exactly what kinds of consumer abuses occur in postsecondary education? From a recent study by the American Institutes for Research (AIR) that analyzed and classified student complaints to the U.S. Office of Education and the Federal Trade Commission, the following list of intentional abuses emerged:[5]

• inequitable refund policies and failure to make timely tuition and fee refunds

4. "The Secrecy Behind the College Board," *New York*, October 7, 1974.

5. *Executive Summary: Improving the Consumer Protection Function in Postsecondary Education* (Washington: Office of Planning, Budgeting, and Evaluation; U.S. Office of Education, April 1977), p. 2.

- misleading recruitment and admissions practices
- false or misleading advertising
- inadequate diclosure in written documents
- inadequate instructional programs
- unqualified instructional staff
- excessive turnover in instructional staff
- inadequate instructional equipment and facilities
- inadequate job-placement services (if promised) and lack of follow-up of graduates
- inadequate student orientation practices
- inadequate housing facilities
- inadequate procedures for keeping student records
- misrepresentation or misuse of chartered, approved, or accredited status
- lack of financial stability

In the same study, the AIR surveyed a random sample of forty-five institutions and concluded "that some potential for student abuse existed in every postsecondary institution in the sample studied."[6]

Further evidence of the prevalence and seriousness of the problem of consumer abuse comes from several recent conferences and reports on the subject. For instance, the Federal Interagency Committee on Education (FICE) concedes that "consumers are being exploited in a variety of educational settings."[7] Talking about federal efforts to protect consumers, the same report says:

> Policies are largely reactive. Information provided to the student is inadequate. Safeguards against outright fraud and simple abuse are weak. Few agencies have systematic procedures for handling complaints from students or parents, or for redressing valid claims. Coordination between the Federal agencies is at an embryonic stage, and the educational community itself has not activated consumer protection concepts or mechanisms where consumer problems exist. Among the Federal departments and agencies, the response to educational consumer problems varies considerably.[8]

Student initiatives

In view of the slow response of the federal government to the problem of consumer abuse in postsecondary education, it is not surprising that a new type of student activism has been emerging on our

6. Ibid., p. 3.
7. *Toward a Federal Strategy for Protection of the Consumer of Education* (Washington: Federal Interagency Committee on Education, July 1975), p. 41.
8. Ibid., p. 1.

campuses. Though not as visible as the protests of the 1960s, this new activism takes many forms and uses a variety of tactics that hold considerable potential for effecting change. Among the types of activities that are being undertaken are the following.

Lobbying. The first student lobbying organizations were the University of California Student Lobby and the Student Association of the State University of New York, Inc., both founded in 1970. Today, there are at least seventy state and systemwide lobbies in forty-five states. On the national level, in addition to the National Student Lobby, the National Student Association is involved in lobbying activities, and an organization of students in independent colleges, COPUS (Coalition of Independent College and University Students), also exists. Lobbying efforts have become one of the main strategies used by students and have produced substantial victories, including increased appropriations for institutions, higher levels of financial aid for students, student representation on institutional governing boards, and guarantees to housing rights.

Research. To support their lobbying activities and to improve institutional evaluations, students are becoming more involved in sophisticated forms of research. The National Student Educational Fund, created in 1973, has received over $200,000 in grants and has produced such documents as the Options Handbooks, a series of three booklets that discuss the needs of prospective students for information and counseling services. In addition, Public Interest Research Groups, which usually deal with broad consumer concerns but also focus on educational issues, are active on many campuses. A case in point is the New York PIRG, which is currently investigating the Educational Testing Service.

Unionization. In several states—including Oregon, Montana, and Maine—students have won the statutory guarantee of third-party status in collective negotiations between faculty and administration. In several other states—including Massachusetts and New York—students are investigating the feasibility of actually forming unions and conducting collective negotiations with the administration. Graduate student unions—through which teaching assistants and research assistants negotiate over their rights as employees—have been part of the campus scene for some time.

Participation in institutional governance. At some institutions, students have become more involved in decision making not just in traditional "student" areas such as fees and services but in all aspects of institutional policy. Frequently they serve on institutional governing boards. This increased participation in the actual governance of the institution gives them greater access to information which formerly might have been hidden from them and thus allows them to apply pressure for needed change.

Demonstrations and strikes. While not as prevalent as during the 1960s, these forms of activism have become slightly more common in the last few years, usually in response to economic issues (i.e., rising college costs) but sometimes in response to broader social issues. One of the largest demonstrations in recent years occurred when 10,000 students from New York institutions marched on the state capitol in Albany to protest budget cuts.

Increased peer counseling. As a remedy to deficiencies in institutional information and counseling services, peer counseling has become popular on many campuses. Students who work part time in the financial aid office, the housing office, the health service, and so forth, are able to draw on their experience to help other students, who often feel more comfortable talking to their peers.

Student evaluation of teaching. At many institutions, scientific surveys are now conducted to obtain student reaction to specific courses and instructors. Responses are then summarized and published. These systematic procedures have generally improved the quality of the information that students use in selecting their courses.

Establishment of student-run services. Students on some campuses have been setting up and operating their own services, including book, record, and food cooperatives; pharmacies; birth control clinics; ambulance services; and bus services. While these enterprises are only peripherally related to education, they are a corrective to alleged exploitation of students by commercial operations.

In undertaking these activities, students are motivated not just by self-interest but by a desire to improve education and to increase access for all students, especially those to whom a college education represents a chance to break out of the prison of poverty. It is to be hoped that these student initiatives will result not in confrontation and conflict but in greater understanding and improved cooperation among all the parties involved in postsecondary education.

Recommendations for further action

Efforts by students have produced many positive changes; but further action must be taken by other groups, including the federal government, state governments, and private agencies. While many academic administrators are resentful of what they regard as intrusion, they must recognize that regulation by external agencies is a reality and is not necessarily to be viewed as an evil. Richard Millard notes that regulation can help "to create the structured conditions under which people and institutions with principles can operate effectively."[9]

The federal government has already taken several steps in the right direction, most notably through Section 493A of the Higher Education Act of 1976, which requires institutions to disseminate information to prospective and enrolled students on financial assistance programs, institutional costs, refund policies, and academic programs. The following recommendations for further action are based in part on the recommendations from two recent conferences on consumer abuse in postsecondary education—both sponsored by the Education Commission of the States (ECS) and by several federal agencies including the Departments of Defense, Labor, and Health, Education, and Welfare, and the Veterans Administration—and from the earlier-mentioned FICE report.[10] These nine recommendations are addressed not only to federal and state governments, but also to institutions.

1. States should adopt the 1973 model legislation proposed by ECS to provide minimum safeguards in refund policies and to establish standards for advertising and recruiting. In addition, specifications for contractual relationships should be adopted, as has already been done in three states.

2. The federal government should establish a single national complaint center. Because no such single agency now exists, students are frequently so confused about where to turn for redress of grievances that they do not bother to voice their complaints at all.

3. The federal government should give greater attention to the private accrediting agencies, to assure that they take consumer needs into account.

4. A Federal Tuition Insurance Corporation should be established to assure that students will be given refunds on their tuition and fees if an institution closes.

9. Education Commission of the States, *Conference Report: Consumer Protection in Postsecondary Education,* ECS Report #53 (Denver: ECS, June 1974).

10. Education Commission of the States, *Report of the Second National Conference,* ECS Report #64 (Denver: ECS, March 1975); ECS Report #53, *Toward a Federal Strategy.*

5. The Institutional Report Form (IRF) developed by the Office of Education's Office of Planning, Budgeting, and Evaluation should be utilized to ascertain whether institutions are meeting consumer needs.

6. Institutions should give greater emphasis to self-assessment, including assessment by students. Use of the IRF would compel institutions to engage in such assessment.

7. Institutions should give greater emphasis to peer counseling, to assure that students get the kind of information they need in a form that is understandable to them.

8. Institutions should try to increase student input at all levels of decision making, to assure that consumer needs are taken into account.

9. Students should be given a greater voice in the operation of the College Board, to assure that this agency—which plays a key role in decisions about both admissions and financial aid allocations—is sensitive to consumer needs.

Harold Howe, former U.S. Commissioner of Education, once asked, "Do our schools serve the needs of students, or is it the other way around?"[11] Many observers of the postsecondary education scene have concluded that the latter has too often been the case. As consumer awareness grows among students, and as institutions come to recognize their responsibilities, the situation is gradually changing. Further efforts on the part of all parties involved are needed if postsecondary education is to live up to its promise for our society.

11. Harold Howe, address delivered to the American Association of University Professors, April 26, 1968.

The University and Career Education: Resolving an Ambiguity

TIMOTHY J. HEALY, S.J.

A SERIOUS AMBIGUITY exists in higher education today regarding career education that is revealed in the question, "Why should colleges concern themselves with career education?" This ambiguity is real and deserves attention.

Some careers, and thus some career education, should not be dealt with in a college or a university.

> • When we come to what Alfred North Whitehead called "technical education," there should be no ambiguity. Technical education is something colleges and universities do well and should continue doing.
> • Other, higher areas in career education, of which medicine is an example, ought to give educators pause. The risk is that the university, in its education for a career or a profession, can so change that career or profession that it destroys it.

A story illustrates the first point. Some years ago, while I was with the City University of New York, the Radio Corporation of America was withdrawing its support from the RCA Institute; the Institute faculty requested that CUNY continue it as a CUNY college. The more we at CUNY listened to the Institute faculty, the more we were awed by what they had accomplished. They taught practical skills, many of which were so sophisticated that they required more than a rudimentary knowledge of college-level electronics and mathematics. The Institute programs were run according to the need of the curriculum, not the traditional academic calendar. If a program needed fourteen weeks, or sixty, it got it, without interruption. A

61

student could start and complete a program, without having to adapt himself to the rhythms of the institution.

Other details of the Institute's operation were intriguing. The faculty ran it; the administrative body was very small (comprised mostly of part-time faculty members), and the staff taught up to thirty hours a week. There was nothing democratic about the Institute's organization. The students were there to learn and the faculty were there to help them get on with it. Discipline was clear and well kept. What social life students chose to organize for themselves was completely outside the control or interest of the faculty. The result was a first-class career education program, in which the faculty practitioners knew what they were talking about and could teach it to the satisfaction of their students for a not insubstantial fee.

In the negotiations, the CUNY representatives told the RCA faculty group that no university faculty could contemplate thirty hours of teaching a week. If CUNY brought the Institute under its umbrella, the first outcome would be the imposition of university rhythms and structures on their teaching, making the entire institution six or seven times more costly than it was. CUNY would in addition probably reduce the Institute's efficiency, as well as its integrity. The university simply could not adapt to the kind of intense teaching that was needed. Thus, the judgment was that CUNY would do far better not to absorb the RCA Institute. We all learned from the exchange that higher education can do marvels, but there are many things it cannot do.

A tradition of education

Moving now to what most of us call career education, let us start with Alfred North Whitehead. His comments on "technical education" are useful and very much to the modern point. One is struck by how easily we slide into the trap of creating opposition where he merely wanted difference.

In *The Aim of Education,* Whitehead describes a tradition of education with which he associates the name of Plato that is built upon literature: if one knows and understands and enjoys the best of what has been written, one is an educated man.

Whitehead goes on to speak of another kind of education—different from, but not opposed to, the Platonic—that he associates with the name of St. Benedict. This education consists of helping men translate their knowledge into practical effect, of aiding men in moving from the perception of the mind to the skill of the hand. Whitehead's genius is understanding that these two thrusts in higher education are not opposed but complementary, that Benedict should and does talk to Plato, that each needs the other.

Whitehead's view is that if we bother to keep some of the rules in "technical education" we need not worry about it being illiberal. These rules are not complex.

Enjoyment and wonder

The first is that all technical education, from agriculture to zoology, from business to medicine, needs insertion in a literary and scientific culture. What marks Whitehead's understanding of this insertion is his insistence that literature yield enjoyment, and science, wonder. It does not matter how much of great literature a student has read, provided that he enjoyed reading it. Whitehead makes the same comment about a student's scientific experience. The student being trained for accounting does not need the kind of depth in science that would qualify him for the practice of chemistry, but he ought to have wrestled with science and achieved some kind of scientific wonder.

Whitehead's second rule of technical education is that its teaching must accent principle, not practice. His reason is not any love of the abstract, but that only an understanding of principle will enable a student to adapt the teaching to his ultimate reality, some ten or twenty years later. No educator would dare claim for any of the subjects he teaches that "this is the way it is, was, and always will be." Except in a doxology, that statement is gibberish. Thus, the onus lies on educators to make certain that our teaching of technical subjects deals with theoretical roots of technical practice, so that students can adapt it for themselves in later years.

The third rule Whitehead gives us is that all teaching of technical subjects, and thus all career education, should promote "the imaginative contemplation of learning." Educators should make sure that both the social and ethical dimensions of principle and practice are made explicit for students; that students are encouraged to reflect on these dimensions; and that they draw at least some tentative conclusions before they finish their education. If technical learning is imaginative, then Benedict's career education is as truly liberating for the minds and souls of students as are the more classical liberal and scientific studies of Plato's aristocratic education.

Totally different from Whitehead's world is the world of career education for the higher professions (which seem to be those that pay more). The university should exercise considerable caution in this world, and some serious self-examination. It is all too possible for involvement with a university to wreck a profession.

Universities deal by preference with training along vertical, not horizontal, lines. Uncomfortable with vagueness, professors deeply prefer precision and close work to overviews. An example of the tension this preference creates is a medical school and its hospital. Into the hospital comes a twelve-year-old who is sick. If, as sometimes happens, the sickness involves only a bug in the blood, then the medical school can produce its expert on bugs in the blood of twelve-year-olds, and all will probably be well. If, as is more often the case, the illness involves the child's parents, his teachers, his friends—the matrix of his world—then the specialist may really do more harm than good. Education for horizontal competence in a university medical school is an accident that is frequently regretted. The university exists for the training of specialists, for the vertical world of expertise; the higher the training, the more specialized the practitioner becomes. The horizontally capable generalist is displaced and discredited and in time will simply disappear.

Disabling a profession

A second great disabling hurt the university can inflict on a profession is to render its practitioners almost incapable of arriving at moral or ethical judgments about the profession, its practices, or its impact on society. All career education demands hard training and the repetition of skilled acts until they become second nature. Nothing can dull the edge of speculation so adequately as routine of drill and training. The student learns to see his coursework as a "tool kit" and reacts to his career in the same way. Busy plumbers are traditionally poor ethicists.

An even more dangerous disabling can occur on the rarified heights of university career education. One high specialty is after all every bit as good as another, and only a fool would try to order a university's professional peaks by importance. To the normal isolation of the specialist is added the academic community's respect for each separate eminence. The result is that the middle ground, the valleys, the interstitial spaces where most of us live, labor, and have our problems are largely ignored. "Once the rockets go up who cares where they come down" is a cruel parody of an interdepartmental memo, but like most parodies it has a base of truth.

American medicine is a good example of a career that has been planned by people who run universities. We have created the finest collection of specialists that the world has ever known. They are, however, specialists, and we have increasing difficulty providing for primary medical care in this richest of countries. In the world of specialists there is no place for the general practitioner, for the man who sees medicine as an art, not as a science. The reduction of the art of medicine to the science of medicine is principally the work of the university. Medicine as science has been reinforced by the practice of the profession. Like the beast with two backs, medicine and the university "turne alwey aboute the earthe in peyne."

A rule of operation

University medicine illustrates a rule of university operation: any art that submits itself to a university must of necessity become a science. The profession now presenting itself to the university's embrace is the law. Judges, attorneys, and legal scholars are calling for longer and more specialized training for attorneys, particularly as they advance in their profession. The locus of this training is almost always a university-based law school.

In 1977 considerable imagination is needed to begin thinking of the law as a science. If, however, the university gets its hands on the legal profession in the same manner and to the same extent it has the medical profession, if the same symbiosis between practice and training holds, in another twenty or thirty years, we may well refer to the science of the law exactly as we refer now to the science of medicine.

For the sake of lawyers and the law, government and the governed, and the academic community's sanity and morals, I hope and pray that this projection is wrong.

Career Planning
for the Liberal Arts Undergraduate

PATRICIA A. WATSON

CAREER COUNSELING is practical support service that is much in demand. Each year at the University of San Diego, the Office of Student Affairs administers an Activities Interest Questionnaire to incoming freshmen. For the last four years, the students' primary interest has been the development of reading, writing, and study skills. Running a close second has been making career decisions and taking career programs. The experience at other colleges and universities has been similar.

What should college and university administrators do to respond to this demand? Establish or increase existing career counseling and placement services. The organization and placement of these services will differ from campus to campus. Some administrators will include a career counselor on the staff of the university counseling center. Others will open a separate office. Some administrators will add career counseling to the centralized placement service. Others will set up a placement office in each university school or college.

However, at the undergraduate level, wherever possible, career counseling and placement should be the responsibility of one office, if for no other reasons that that the business community prefers to deal with a single office and maintaining two career libraries is costly of time and effort.

Other factors require joining the two. The process of career counseling and placement is a continuum; to distinguish one from the other is arbitrary and illogical. Career counselors rightly place the student at the center of the process. However, career counselors who are out of touch with the business community fail to recognize that while a student wants self-fulfillment from a job, the employer wants function-fulfillment. Further, counselors should recognize, as do placement officers, that a tight labor market limits occupational opportunities. A placement officer can make the opposite mistake of placing the occupation at the center of the process, negating the work of the career counselor. Career counseling and placement should therefore exist in one office to meet the needs of both the student and the employer.

Let us presume that a single career counseling and placement office exists and that it is fully staffed. What kinds of activities occur there? The student entering college in 1978 was born in 1961; he or she will retire at age sixty-five, in the year 2026. Consider the changes that have taken place in society in the fifty years between 1925 and 1975 that have affected the religious, social, and moral frameworks for human living. Now think of the changes likely to occur between 1975 and 2025. Students are understandably uncertain about the future. Instead of inheriting values, students now must create their own. Helping clarify these values is a primary task of career counselors. Does the student prefer the material values of profit, security, status, and wealth or the humanitarian values of service and leadership? Does he or she prefer independence, opportunity, and adventure or power, authority, and stability?

In addition to the occupational role, the student will live other roles. For example, he values being a husband and father and she values being a wife and mother and both value profit, so both work. A job opportunity opens that pays $100 more per month than a current position but requires an extra hour a day in commuting time. Which value applies?

Developing self-concept

The student must also examine moral values. Suppose he or she values honesty and integrity and security, and there is a job-related conflict between integrity and security. Which value applies? Values clarification is important in developing self-concept, which is implemented through career development.

Another important aspect of career counseling is skills identification. Perhaps the resumé of the future should state that a prospective employee can analyze, communicate, persuade, plan and organize, reason numerically, and develop goals. Another can identify issues, meet deadlines, pay attention to detail, manage, and summarize. Still another can motivate, cooperate, and supervise. Change is the only certainty in preparing students to participate in the work world of the future. Flexibility is an essential requirement of a career counseling program. Yet students fear flexibility and want guarantees the career counselor cannot give. The counselor can remove much of the fear of flexibility by helping students realize that each person has the potential for success in a number of occupations because of the transferability of intellectual skills.

Another career counseling reality relates to the institutions surrounding the student. There is no substitute for work experience in helping an individual develop career goals. For this reason the career counseling and placement office must be involved in generating part-time and summer employment opportunities, in the business and the university communities. Unfortunately, many career counselors miss the work opportunities available on campus in co-op or internship programs. Too often, faculty members and administrators complain, "You can't count on students during exams; they are not accurate; they cannot keep their minds on the job; they don't show up." If true, these are devastating statements, for a university that is unhappy with the job performance of its own students cannot expect anyone else to hire them. To counter this attitude, career counselors should promote the work habits of promptness, dependability, accuracy, and productivity in work-study programs.

Career counselors recognize that many students come to college with no clear career plans. About half of those students who do have plans change them as a result of their experience with the curriculum. Counselors work with most of these students to help them sort out goals—with individual students, with groups of students with common interests, or during noncredit seminars. But some students are much more lost than others. Frequently these are bright students who enjoy many academic disciplines and cannot bring themselves to commit to an academic major, much less a career plan.

Credit for career and life planning course

To assist these students, career counseling and placement personnel should offer formal courses in career/life planning. A one-semester, three-hour-a-week course does not seem to be an excessive investment for a student to explore personal, societal, and corporate values; understand the relationships of interests and personality to occupational choice; evaluate skills; cover occupational information; and learn job-seeking skills. The community colleges offer excellent career courses. In some four-year colleges, offering such courses for credit is resisted because counseling is not considered an academic discipline and cannot be credited. A possible way to circumvent this resistance is to find a department or school that will list the course to be taught by career counselors. The problem with that solution is that the student who has not declared a major finds the course accidentally, if at all. Yet, when students do find these courses, they appreciate them. Excerpts from student evaluations of a career/life planning course offered last spring at the University of San Diego illustrate the point.

1. I feel very lucky that I have had the opportunity to take Career/Life Planning. . . . I feel the course is probably the most important one I will ever take because it has helped me to really get in touch with myself.
2. This course was excellent in every way. I would highly recommend it for every college student. In fact, it should be a requirement.
3. A stimulating, provocative course; a real "upper." I have never worked harder or derived more from a course.
4. I feel that Career/Life Planning is an excellent class especially for undeclared majors. If one gets nothing else out of the class he will find he likes (himself or herself) a lot better.

The student vote is in. Convincing members of the faculty and the curriculum committee of the value of such courses is another matter.

The career counselor must also be prepared to deal with the special problems of different segments of the student population, for example, women. The U.S. Census Bureau recently reported that the number of women attending colleges has reached a record high of 47 percent of the total.

Reconciling conflicts

The difficulty in counseling young women is reconciling two sometimes seemingly conflicting careers. Gail Sheehy in *Passages* states: "Yet even today, sociologists report that many women between the ages of eighteen and twenty-four live as if suspended. They can't bring themselves to make career commitments, or any extended plan for that matter, until they know whom they are going to marry."[1] In effect, career counseling for young women is also marriage counseling.

Of the women currently in college, the Census Bureau states that 489,000 are thirty-five years old or older. In this category is the married woman, with children, who has been out of school about fifteen years and who is preparing to contribute financially to the family. Naturally her academic skills are rusty and she lacks self-confidence. She prob-

1. *Passages: Predictable Crises of Adult Life* (New York: Bantam Books, 1977), p. 101.

ably also feels guilty; the return to school makes homemaking a part-time job. Something has to give at home—cooking or cleaning or less time with the family; resentment and guilt feelings follow.

The special problems of women students exemplify that career counseling and placement personnel must possess broad professional training in counseling as the undergirding for specific work in career counseling or placement.

The staff in the career counseling and placement center, in addition to daily tasks, should also explore ways to integrate career counseling into academic programs. I am not advocating the creation of courses in career math or career English, but, rather, the promotion of an awareness throughout the campus of the need for students to develop transferrable skills, especially in communication and computation. A 1974 study of employer attitudes and opinions regarding college graduates found that the academic characteristic most directly related to employment is the student's major, and that liberal arts majors are generally regarded as neutral or somewhat undesirable by most employer groups. These students' employment chances would be improved by courses or academic minors in accounting, mathematics, economics, or business.[2] Similarly, a new student guidebook, "Exploring Careers in Humanities," points out that our society is generating more and more data that must be organized and analyzed. Humanities majors who include computer use and statistics in their studies will have the best chances for employment.[3]

In addition to cognitive skills, students need to develop certain behavioral skills. People get and progress in jobs, or do not get or lose jobs as much on their ability or inability to get along with people as on their ability to do a job. Psychology courses for the nonpsychology major that cover theories of personality and human relations would benefit any student seeking a job.

Cognitive and behaviorial skills are already covered in college and university curricula. What is needed is an awareness among students of the career implications inherent in the disciplines these courses

2. Jane L. Anton and Michael L. Russell, *Employer Attitudes and Opinions Regarding Potential College Graduate Employees* (Stanford: Western College Placement Association, 1974), p. 5.

3. Jean Workman, *Exploring Careers in the Humanities: A Student Guidebook,* Technical Education Research Centers, Inc. (Washington: Government Printing Office, 1976), p. 4.

reflect and a willingness among faculty members to provide and teach accounting, economics, mathematics, business, statistics, computer science, and psychology to students not majoring in them.

A fundamental question

Donald K. Smith of the University of Wisconsin goes beyond specifics to ask a fundamental question, Are colleges and universities in fact teaching the skills of language and number that will provide students with currently useful competencies and the capacity for further learning?[4] He states that faculty and administrators have been reluctant to tell either students or the public that certain liberal arts skills are prerequisite to the baccalaureate degree, and that it will no longer be awarded to persons who do not demonstrate competence in those skills. Smith believes that both public opinion of and student satisfaction with higher education would change markedly if we were able to state that minimally a degree from a particular university meant that the recipient had command of certain intellectual skills. Perhaps the best way to integrate career counseling into the curriculum is to identify the cognitive skills liberal arts should provide and then to insist that the students master them.

Career counseling and placement probably does not receive the recognition it deserves on many college campuses. Yet no more important office is involved in retaining students, especially in the current climate of doubt about the value of a college education.

Career counselors also face frustrations in the business community. Never are there enough part-time jobs available to students. Neither are there enough entry-level career opportunities for students completing four years of college.

Career counseling and placement has its rewards. When a student begins to understand who he is, his eyes light up because he likes that person. When a student begins to realize that she has marketable skills, she smiles because she is proud of them. When they both develop confidence from learning the proper techniques to get not only that entry-level job but also the five or six others they will have during their lifetime, career counselors and placement officers know the worth of their work.

4. Donald K. Smith, "What's a Liberal Education Coming to?" *Wisconsin Ideas* (May 1976).

Career Development Through Job Competency Assessment

GEORGE O. KLEMP, JR.

THE IDEA OF A CAREER suggests a lifelong dedication to a particular endeavor. Most people consider a career to be a profession, requiring preparation and training and undertaken as a calling. Career planning, accordingly, is very serious. Our choices of educational experiences, when we are fortunate enough to have such choices, lead us toward a narrowing field of desirable career alternatives. The immutability of some early decisions propels many students along well-worn and predictable career paths quite without their will; these decisions are reinforced, if not prompted, by career counselors who exhort the student to be "realistic" about his or her abilities and aspirations. It is small wonder that a career change is traumatic, whether the change is initiated by or forced onto us.

Defining a career as a profession is not the most useful way to express the concept. Rather, a career is a course along which one may be expected to progress. A career is not merely a profession or series of related jobs; it is a set of work events to which an individual contributes uniquely, a series of jobs that need have no link other than that which the individual—with his or her skills, knowledge, and abilities—provides.

By this definition of career, we focus not on the requirements of particular jobs but on *competencies,* or the general abilities and characteristics by which a person performs effectively in a wide range of occupations. Recently, McBer and Company identified the competencies of successful practitioners in service, technical, and administrative professions, who work in a variety of public and private-sector careers. Through this identification process, or *job competence assessment,* we have learned much about the kinds of knowledge, skills, abilities, and characteristics that are related to superior performance.

Job competence assessment

Job competence assessment is based on several assumptions.

1. *The ability to perform the tasks in a job description does not by itself guarantee a high level of performance.* A job task analysis,

for example, might identify taking measurements and writing reports as being primary aspects of job content. Selecting a person with superior writing and mathematical skills might seem the best way to ensure effective performance when logical thinking ability and task efficiency may be far more important attributes. The knowledges and skills related to job tasks are necessary for the minimum performance of a particular job but may not themselves be sufficient for effective performance. Thus, one must consider both the tasks to be performed in a job and the characteristics of the performer in the job competence equation.

2. *The best way to identify job competence is to find individuals who are outstandingly successful in their work and then analyze what they do.* Rather than relying on experts' assertions about the most important traits of the successful performer, the job competence assessment method relies primarily on observing the individual performer on the job, without reference to the factors held to be important. The assumption is that the successful incumbent is the expert on what it takes to do the job well.

3. *The most efficient way to identify job competence is first to analyze the performance of people in the most senior positions.* The competencies of senior professionals, from our experience, best reflect the strengths and values of an organization. Subsequent analyses of individuals in other positions can be related to the analysis of people higher in the organization to identify competency requirements for all jobs. In most cases, senior incumbents possess a greater variety of skills and abilities than their less experienced colleagues, so their competencies are more readily applicable to lower-level jobs than are the competencies of lower-level incumbents to senior positions.

Job competence assessment incorporates job task analysis procedures but differs from standard job analysis in two important respects. First, it compares performers judged exemplary on one or more criteria and typical performers, while other approaches take the average performer as the standard for analysis. Second, an interview based on Flanagan's critical incident technique[1] is used to reconstruct an incumbent's behaviors that contribute to effective and ineffective job performance. This technique provides the researcher with the recollection of experience rather than inferences about what made a particu-

1. John C. Flanagan, "The Critical Incident Technique, *Psychological Bulletin* 51 (1954): 327–58.

lar outcome successful or unsuccessful; the data are also behaviorally organized so the researcher can compare superior and average job incumbents. These two features of the job competence assessment process reveal the knowledge, abilities, skills, and characteristics that comprise adequate job performance as well as those abilities that predict outstanding performance.

Career planning and competency

McBer and Company has conducted job competence assessments of career professionals at many levels. Although these studies do not represent a true cross section of careers, a number of findings related to career planning and development are remarkably consistent across organizations.

Many competencies required by senior and mid-career specialists are identical. Within specific areas of professional endeavor, the competencies that relate to outstanding performance are the same in positions at the senior and the mid-career levels; the only difference is that successful senior specialists have developed these competencies to a higher degree. Regardless of level, scientists and researchers, for example, must be able to conceptualize; human services professionals must relate well with people; managers must be able to plan; and administrators must be able to lead. The optimum combination of these and other competencies remains consistent in its relationship to effective performance as professionals advance in their careers.

The most senior positions in any organization tend to be multifunctional and the competencies needed are usually a combination of specialist competencies. Anyone who aspires to senior positions should acquire all the competencies needed in specialty and in other jobs that overlap the senior generalist positions. Students who have decided on a career area should follow this same path, whether they aspire to the top positions or not, since the competencies required in these are also important to success in many others. Career planning that includes acquiring these key competencies therefore broadens an individual's job choices.

Specialized knowledge beyond that which is required for minimal performance does not distinguish the superior performer. Many education institutions are bound to the assumption that knowledge and career competence are directly related, as reflected in the use of the grade-point average as a summary of a student's capability.

The relationship between knowledge and competence holds to a certain point; one cannot perform adequately if one does not possess the minimum knowledge to do a job. Present evidence indicates, however, that knowledge level does not account for the differences between the superior and the average performer, even in the most technical occupations and professions.[2] In addition, the evidence indicates that most of the specialized knowledge required in many careers can be learned on the job. Many careers demand a high degree of specialized knowledge as a prerequisite for successful performance, but many careers do not require any greater knowledge than can be gained in a year of job training. Indeed, much specialized knowledge *must* be acquired on the job, since liberal arts curricula do not provide the specificity needed in the entry-level jobs that liberal arts graduates are most likely to take.

The ability to learn new material quickly appears to be more important than the knowledge one has already acquired. If a student is quick to learn, he or she need not be directed away from pursuing a career area because of insufficient knowledge. Skills training, therefore, is an inefficient way to ensure career competence. There are surely other, more basic abilities that a liberal arts education develops in providing foundation for personal growth.

Many important entry-level competencies actually hinder career advancement. The first jobs college graduates accept in their careers are usually individual contributor jobs. These require applying specialized skills, many of which are learned in on-the-job or related training, to provide a service or otherwise add value to a product. The person who can concentrate for long periods on one task, enjoys direct involvement with the task, attends to details, is efficient, and can work without supervision may be a very effective contributor. Most jobs beyond the entry level, however, require work management, cooperation with others, delegation, planning, and interpersonal influence. Many competencies of the successful individual contributor will become less important and may even become obstacles to career growth as the career opportunity horizon widens. In support of this, our research reveals that outstanding individual contributors are often passed over in promotion in favor of other, seemingly less competent individuals; for those who are promoted a number of the competen-

2. David C. McClelland, "Testing for Competence Rather Than for 'Intelligence,'" *American Psychologist* 28 (1973): 1–14.

cies they possess may be inappropriate for their first jobs but are noticed by supervisors as indicators of high performance potential in later jobs.

A current trend among many colleges which consists of the increased use of entry-level career acceptability as the criterion to determine whether or not students have been prepared adequately for their careers. The present findings suggest that a longer view of student career preparation and counseling is needed. Education institutions should at least make students cognizant of the competencies they will need later in their careers.

Specialists are generally not promoted to top administrative or managerial positions. The difference between the generalist and the specialist is that the generalist, while sharing much technical knowledge and intellectual ability with the specialist, can also lead and manage. The few specialists who have found their way to top positions without competencies in leadership and management are the exceptions; usually they are surrounded by people who possess complementary competencies. Persons who are taking their first steps in formal career planning, as well as those who are considering a mid-life career change, should recognize some of the career development limitations that may result from specializing.

During the years to come, colleges may need to address the issues relating to specialist versus generalist career education. In terms of career opportunity, students who concentrate exclusively on becoming good technicians may some day be at a considerable disadvantage compared with peers who are better versed in leadership and management. In many of the organizations in which we conducted job competency assessment, technical capability had long been emphasized as the principal indicator of an individual performer's ability; our analyses showed that this emphasis has no empirical support. Beyond technical skill, a variety of interpersonal and managerial skills and abilities are needed for successful performance in senior positions that are seldom indicated in the liberal arts curriculum. These include diagnostic listening, persuasive communication, understanding human motivation, planning, group processing, logical thinking, and problem solving.[3] Some of the best career counseling one can give an individual would be that he or she acquire the widest

3. George O. Klemp, Jr., "Three Factors of Success," in *Relating Work and Education,* ed. D. Vermilye (San Francisco: Jossey-Bass, 1977).

possible repertoire of competencies that are needed in top positions. Colleges, however, must first reevaluate their curricular goals to ensure that some of these competencies are developed during the course of an undergraduate education.

No single entry or mid-career position adequately prepares a person for senior generalist positions. A recent job competency assessment of outstanding senior professionals uncovered two types of mid-level professionals: administrators, whose strongest competencies were interpersonal and managerial, and technicians, whose primary strengths were intellectual. One finding was that neither the technical professionals nor the administrative professionals possessed all the competencies needed for successful performance in the senior management positions. However, most of the outstanding senior incumbents had prepared themselves for their present jobs by moving through different jobs that developed the missing competencies.

Professional development, then, may be achieved as effectively through experience in other mid-career positions as through training. A successful career planning strategy should include more than academic preparation or training. Few students, indeed few professionals, are aware of the alternatives available to them for developing competencies that will bring them closer to their career goals. The specialist who wishes to become more of a generalist would do well to gain multifunctional experience through a progression of horizontal job changes rather than immediately moving up within a specialty. Students who are preparing for generalist careers through a specialty should also consider horizontal movement through different specialist jobs as a way to acquire the competencies needed in senior positions.[4]

Prescriptions for career guidance

Our research strongly suggests that career success is a function of an appropriate mix of interdependent competencies. Career planning and development, however, tend to distinguish among specific knowledges, skills, and abilities as if they were independent of each other and could be gained separately, like pieces of a puzzle. Job descriptions and task analyses have so pervaded career consciousness that most people may be concerned more with matching their skills to those required by the task and less with their ability to grow with

4. Richard N. Bolles, *What Color Is My Parachute?* (Berkeley: Ten Speed Press, 1972).

a job and to augment it. Job competence assessment provides information for more effective individual career planning and development. The outcome is not just a list of individual competencies but a picture of how and why they interact in particular careers, and is thus a guide for designing education and training experiences that reinforce that interaction. Though job competence assessment emphasizes those competencies that lead to effective performance in a given job, its goal is the development of individuals over the course of a career. It goes beyond job definition by identifying standards for different levels of performance and is therefore aimed at long-term performance improvement for the individual and the organization.

A shared responsibility

The successful match of a person to a career is a responsibility shared by the individual, the college, the employer, and the career counselor. Job competence assessment suggests how the employer and the career counselor can help achieve such a match as students begin their careers. Employers, to facilitate employee career development, could publicize the competencies required in top positions. Making these competencies known can motivate incumbents in junior and intermediate positions and direct their attention to those competencies that will lead to advancement, special training, and other career opportunities. They may even decide whether or not the particular careers they are pursuing are for them. An added dividend of publicizing competency requirements is that performance and promotion criteria are made explicit so employees can compare their own performance at different career points with that of successful senior career professionals. An employee's interest in training also tends to change when these criteria are known, from improving performance in the present job to learning the skills of the next job. Not all future professionals will work in large organizations, and many will even be self-employed, which only increases the student's responsibility for finding out what competencies are important for effective performance.

An individual seeking career counseling needs to know his or her capabilities match the requirements of a prospective job as well as those of future positions. By stressing competencies rather than job descriptions, career counselors can suggest a better match between a person's present capabilities and the competencies required in various career options. This kind of career planning goes beyond skills assessment. For example, college students seeking placement may be evaluated for interpersonal, managerial, or leadership capabilities, which they have not had measured before. But for the liberal arts undergraduate, a successful evaluation in these competencies may have more meaning in the world of work than a successful record in his or her academic major. A second area in which career counseling can benefit the student is competency development. The counselor can suggest particular courses, jobs, or other learning opportunities that will enable the student to develop generic competencies that will augment long-term career effectiveness.

Job and life effectiveness

What can the individual do to build an appropriate foundation of competencies? The competencies that enable a person to excel in a particular job also enable that person to be effective in other areas of life. It follows that the same competencies that are important to a career may be developed in noncareer activities. In the classroom, in the residence hall, in extracurricular interests, and in part-time employment, college students demonstrate intellectual, interpersonal, leadership, and managerial competencies that are not reflected in a transcript but that nevertheless contribute to career performance. For example, the study of philosophy sharpens conceptual ability; being a dormitory counselor enhances the ability to empathize; serving in student government develops persuasive communication; and working for a student newspaper or radio station reinforces both communication and time-management skills. This perspective of competency attainment can also provide insight into a student's reasons for taking a leave of absence from college and what he or she hopes to gain from such an experience. A career counseling service that encompasses the total undergraduate experience would help the student realize a more realistic yet broadening set of career opportunities. Such a service could also suggest cocurricular experiences for developing important competencies that would complement and supplement the curriculum.

A competency, as it has been defined, is a generic concept that underlies the organization of skills and their effective application. For example, a person will not be an effective communicator, regardless of his or her speaking skill, if certain competencies are lacking, such as the ability to conceptualize and think logically, needed to define and organize a presentation or the ability to influence the audience. But the same competencies that underlie specific communication skills are the foundation of many other skills as well; thus the power of generic competencies exceeds that of skills and even that of a specific knowledge base. The implications of job competence assessment for career planning and development, then, are clear: focusing on generic competencies, rather than on specific skills, and on a career as a series of broadening experiences, rather than as a sequence of jobs, provides the student and the education institution with a link between the world of college and the world of work.

Standards Versus Opportunity:
The Unnecessary Conflict

JOHN R. SILBER

IT IS ESSENTIAL that all of us in higher education—faculty, students, administrators—realize that any intelligent discussion of standards must acknowledge that a revolution has taken place in education. We have opened the classroom to persons of such diverse talent and ability that the application of the traditional grading scale raises very serious problems. When we admit anyone who has attained an eighth-grade education—and this is the standard now being urged to tighten open-admissions standards at the City University of New York—we admit students who cannot possibly do passing work in the context of traditional standards. I do not mean that all students admitted under such a standard are bound to fail. Some, through dedication and intensive remedial work, can succeed. That they can succeed amply justifies open admissions and intensive remediation. But many others cannot, and concern for equal opportunity should not lead us to graduate them without regard to whether they have been educated. There is no conflict between reasonable academic standards and open admission. But it is impossible to maintain standards while allowing automatic graduation. To increase educational opportunity the standards of admission may be compromised. But if the standards for graduation are compromised, the integrity of higher education will be destroyed.

Serious damage was imposed on academic standards by the Vietnam war and the government policy of draft deferments for students. Such deferments represented class legislation that was a throwback to the days of the Civil War when the affluent could hire substitutes to be drafted in their place. The government bestowed an advantage on the children of the middle class that was all too often denied minority youths. These young people, lacking financial and sometimes cultural and social opportunities for college attendance, were shipped directly to Vietnam without being able to plead benefit of clergy.

But the advantage bestowed on the others was ambivalent. After 1965, professors began to be faced with new pressures to dilute standards. Students had always wheedled for grades, but now they confronted the professor with a terrible alternative: Give me a C or send me to Vietnam, possibly to my death. Faculty with impaired ethical judgment did not realize that when they flunked such a student, they were not sending him to Vietnam but were rather giving him the privilege of facing up to or evading his own moral and political responsibilities. It was still up to the student to decide: Should he accept military service? Should he claim conscientious-objector status? Should he accept service but refuse to go to Vietnam? Or should he flee to Canada? When faculty issued perjured grades to relieve students from moral responsibility, they patronized them, treating them as less than responsible adults.

The larger society suffered from the deferment system even more than the students, for it denied the United States an early warning of the lack of support for the war. If, in 1964, the children of the professional class had been subject to death in Vietnam, it is unlikely that the massive buildup of U.S. forces in 1965 would have happened. The parents would have stopped the war and not left it to the children, who, in their attempt to end the war, launched a misguided and destructive crusade against the university itself.

And so the increased presence of students who could meet no reasonable criteria of performance and the pressures of Vietnam conspired to relax standards. At the same time, a general relaxation of basic integrity was signaled by the rise of companies that made a business of producing term papers. Faculty and administration all too often complacently accepted the operation of these academic well-poisoners, so that even where reasonable standards of performance were maintained, it became easier to meet them through fraud. Such companies, which had always been a marginal pestilence in the academy, began to flourish as faculty no longer knew enough of their students' abilities and eccentricities to recognize plagiarized work when they saw it. Worse, many faculties refused to administer more than a slap on the wrist—if that much—to students who were caught using plagiarized papers.

The decline of standards

All of these trends contributed heavily to the phenomenon of grade inflation. In the decade following 1965, the average grade nationally rose from $C+$ to $B-$. Some have defended inflated grades as an accurate measurement of the performance of a superior generation of students who surpass their less gifted predecessors. But the evidence accumulates that entering students are less prepared than ever, that distinguished colleges must offer remedial reading work to many of their freshmen, and that more and more college graduates are functional illiterates. All measures available to us except the inflated grades themselves contradict the notion that today's students are the best and the brightest. Indeed, taking the entire student population into consideration, by opening access we have stated as a policy that students should *not* be only the best and brightest. We may well as a matter of policy extend access to everyone, but we should never maintain fraudulently that everyone will perform equally well.

The present difficulty in applying standards is not limited to open-access community colleges. The educational issue raised in Bakke vs. California is the critical need for the development of adequately sophisticated admissions standards. Had the University of California developed criteria of evaluation that took into account the educational deprivation experienced by the poor of all races and moderated its reliance on Medical College Admission Test and other scores through careful personal evaluation of applicants, there could have been little reason for intervention by the courts. Instead, the university retained a numerological basis for admission for most students and then allowed sixteen minority applicants to use their skin color or surname as substitutes for the numbers.

As long as faculties wish to avoid serious assessment of applicants and rely instead on the numerology of the Law School Admission Test, the Medical College Admission Test, and other tests, they leave themselves open to charges of reverse discrimination. It should be clear that, while not all affirmative action programs involve reverse discrimination, when reverse discrimination does exist it is as indefensible as the traditional kind. It is racist to deal with people as members of races rather than as individuals—at any time, in any place, for any reason. The United States is at long last rejecting racism as a basis for organizing its society, and the academy will make a terrible mistake if it encourages an atavistic policy of reverse discrimination.

As it happens, Boston University has one of the best records on equal opportunity of any institution in the United States. From our founding all our programs have been open to both sexes, all races, all religions, and we were the first university to reject all discrimination on the grounds of sex and race. But we have never admitted or graduated minority students on the basis of adulterated standards. We could not have thus condescended to such applicants as Barbara Jordan or Martin Luther King, because it would be a form of racism to lower standards for minority students. We develop sophisticated means for evaluating applicants who have been shortchanged in their earlier education and sophisticated programs of orientation and counseling for them after they arrive. But the university assumes that they are intellectually the equal of white students and expects them over the long term to perform as well.

If we educators insist on treating ability as something that can be measured adequately by the Scholastic Aptitude Test, there is a serious conflict between standards and affirmative action. But if we consider ability in a reasonably complex and profound sense, there need be no compromises between standards and affirmative action. We have long accepted the principle of adding points to veterans' civil service exam scores. As long as there is other evidence as to ability, I see no difficulty in adding points to the Scholastic Aptitude Test score of someone from a seriously inadequate high school. We ought to be encouraging research to ascertain what would be a reasonable number of points to add, merely as a corrective of a score that does not adequately measure actual ability. As long as there is evidence of keen intelligence and high motivation, there is no reason why we should not discount an inadequate standardized test. But we should not make the mistake of assuming that all disadvantaged students will do badly on standardized tests. At the University of Texas, I know a black student from a poor town whose mother was a charwoman. He came from a family whose economic and educational background was seriously inadequate, yet he scored higher than 600 on both parts of the SAT. The explanation was that his mother was highly motivated, passed that motivation on to her son, and made sure that he was put into the hands of a superb teacher in his high school. And so he came to college with advanced placement in English, mathematics, and Russian.

At the other extreme, we had a white graduate student who had graduated from a demanding philosophy program at Notre Dame with straight A's. But his combined score on the Graduate Record Examination was only 700. It took an immense amount of work to get him admitted to a Master's program at Texas, where he performed brilliantly; he then took a Ph.D. at Yale and published a book at the same time he completed his dissertation. Any university that relied heavily on Graduate Record Examination scores would have ignored him, even though he was as surely a victim of numerological standards as any minority student.

There is certainly no necessary compromise between affirmative action and standards unless one adopts the patently racist or sexist view that racial minorities or women really are inferior. Excellence—comprehensively understood—can be required of all groups protected by affirmative action.

Strengthening standards

At the graduate level, the relaxation of standards has led to the harassment of faculty to a degree that suggests we have started on the road back to Bologna, with students believing that they hire the faculty to service them as they please. Pressures to remove the language requirement and to weaken the comprehensive examinations for the Ph.D. reflect an increasing student reluctance to accept reasonable professional standards. To refuse to learn a foreign language is to insist on remaining imprisoned in a single culture. To refuse comprehensive examinations is to refuse to be tested on any other basis than the one-night cram. It is to refuse to be tested on the residue of knowledge growing out of years of study. The alternative is the reductionistic exam that offers no subtle or effective testing of one's abilities. It is unfortunate enough that such exams are used to admit students; it is seriously disturbing when they are used, as they now sometimes are, to offer college credit or to establish candidacy for graduate degrees.

If we in higher education are able to achieve grade deflation, the effect on marginal students can only be salutary. We will start being honest with them. Instead of certifying students fraudulently for a life for which they are ill-equipped, we will encourage a career suited to their abilities. Far better to be a well-educated plumber, happy with your work, than a dyspeptic professor of English who doesn't much like to read and who cannot write. It is important for us to realize that grade inflation is a species of fraud, and one from which ultimately no one but those who inflate the grades can profit, and their profit is gained in a sleazy business.

Over the short term standards are seriously threatened by a climate of shrinking student enrollment. It is likely that some independent and state-supported colleges, in order to delay their decline a few years, will adopt a policy of automatic admission, automatic retention, and automatic graduation. They will be able to purchase a few years of life but at the cost of all their principles. As long as some degree of certification still inheres in degrees offered by such colleges, they will draw students who are interested merely in certification rather than education.

It is a likely consequence that the abuses attendant on such circumstances will utterly devalue the certification implicit in a college degree. The states will then be forced to establish agencies to assess the abilities of students independently of their education and to award or deny certification. If this happens, higher education will find itself out of the certification business entirely and will have the opportunity to turn its attention toward providing the kind of experience and education upon which maximum human development must depend. Thus, through a surprising reversal, a superficially threatening chain of events may, at the end, save the integrity of the academic community.

Assessing Quality, Excellence, and Honesty

JOSEPH N. HANKIN

Our legacy of holocausts and dislocations have left us confused about limits, no longer certain about where anything begins or ends. . . . Our response to the crisis of boundaries is a desperate attempt to hold fast to all existing categories, to keep all definitions pure. This is, unfortunately, the impulse of a great world, including that of classical Marxism and classical psychoanalysis. More than being merely conservative, this response is a reaction to a perceived threat of chaos; it all too readily lends itself to nostalgic visions of restoring a golden age of exact boundaries, an age in which men allegedly knew exactly where they stood. The approach is self-defeating and, moreover, impossible to maintain.[1]

AN EXAMINATION of the catalogs of institutions of higher learning is both revealing and confusing. Virtually every one of them has a long list of goals for students to attain by the end of their education. The correlation between the written word and the actual accomplishment is not always measurable; nor, for the most part, is any such measurement even attempted.

The question of academic standards has always been a persistent theme in higher education. St. Augustine and even Socrates before him complained about their students' performance. Throughout time individuals have harkened back to a golden age when all was well. Leslie Fiedler, noted American literary critic and chairperson of the department of English at the State University of New York at Buffalo, recently remarked that, at his first faculty meeting in the 1930s, the members of the instructional staff were complaining about the deterioration in the quality of written expression. An article of that era observed: "of course, we all know that many 'students' pass examination and still know nothing about the subject."[2]

The arguments continue in the present. On the one hand, some argue that students are brighter than ever before; on the other hand, some contend that there are masses of unqualified students who denigrate the meaning of a higher education. The vociferous critics are not an insignificant minority. According to supercritic Peter Witonski, for example, higher education has stooped so low that "an earned degree from many of our accredited colleges and universities is often not worth much more than a degree purchased from a diploma mill."[3] He goes on to observe that:

> If one appends to the officially recognized [sic] diploma mills, the hundreds of unaccredited institutions that are not so recognized, and the thousand or so accredited institutions that really offer little more in the way of an education than the unaccredited schools, one begins to appreciate the extent of the problem confronting the students in

1. Robert Lifton, *Boundaries: Psychological Man in Revolution* (New York: Random House, 1969), Introduction.

2. Patricia R. Foster, "Education Grows Up," *College Humor* (March 1971), p. 7.

3. *What Went Wrong with American Education and How to Make it Right* (New Rochelle, New York: Arlington House, 1973), p. 108.

search of a genuine education today. It all boils down to the fact that American educators have been so lax about standards for so long a time that they have come to tolerate the existence even of the wretched diploma mills, often citing them as being "innovative" or "experimental."[4]

Everyone concerned with higher education is aware of the presence of diploma mills. By latest count there are several hundred such bogus institutions. Terence H. Bell, former United States Commissioner of Education, in a study of diploma mills, defined one as ". . . an organization that awards degrees without requiring its students to meet educational standards for such degrees established and traditionally followed by reputable educational institutions."[5] This, then, makes it easy for us to recognize institutions that are substandard! Or does it?

The old standards

What are these commonly accepted standards? Can the colleges, the employers, the students, the transfer and graduate institutions agree on standards at all? Can they agree on some measurable criteria for assessing institutional quality, such as:

- achievement test and entrance examination scores of applicants
- quality point indices of students
- attrition (or length of time needed to obtain a degree)
- percentage of students continuing into graduate education
- percentage of students scoring over a certain grade on the College-Level Examination Program, Graduate Record Examination, or other standardized tests
- number of books, basic and rare
- equipment in laboratories and studios
- number of square feet devoted to instructional activities
- student-faculty ratios
- number of student and faculty honors
- percentage of faculty members with the earned doctorate
- number of faculty publications

4. Ibid.

5. Terence H. Bell, "Dimensions for Effectiveness in Education," address before the Joint Annual Meeting of the Northwest Association of Schools and Colleges, the North West Association of Community and Junior Colleges, and the Western College Association (Reno, Nevada, December 9, 1975).

- grants obtained by faculty members
- depth of involvement of faculty is decisionmaking
- cost per student

There is little question that if educators can agree on an appropriate yardstick, then most of these factors can be measured fairly efficiently. They are, however, quantities that are often qualities that students arrive with rather than being added later. If we are not measuring the results of the education process, how do we know that we are fulfilling our purpose? The management consultant Peter Drucker has made the distinction that efficiency is doing things right, while effectiveness is doing the right things. To what extent have we been focusing on the right things? Many of the factors typically chosen for measurement have been suspect for some time, yet we cling tenaciously to their measurement, perhaps because they *can* be measured, and they *have* been measured, rather than because they *should* be measured.

Let us look briefly at some of these typical standards and norms. Educators' attention should be focused on moving away from these more commonly measurable factors to what may be described as less tangible, but perhaps more meaningful accomplishments.

One of the first measures of quality is selectivity in admissions. There are those who see a drastic decline in quality since the onset of open admissions and full opportunity programs, which permit virtually any high school graduate (and even some who have not finished high school) to attend institutions of higher education. Failing to recognize that admission was always open to those who could afford to pay the bill (regardless of their intellectual capacity), opponents of open admissions decry the fact that greater proportions of students with less ability are being offered the opportunity to enroll in programs that were previously more exclusive. Critics question what is happening to academic standards that now allow almost anyone to be admitted to college; they lament the dilution of standards for graduation and the transfer to remedial programs of money that might otherwise be spent on other institutional priorities.

Advocates of open admissions point out that traditional admissions standards favor students with an economic and social advantage, that the college and university must educate more than the academic elite. They claim that success in educating students of great ability is due less to the quality of the institutions than to the qualities of the students and that those institutions that admit students of lower ability should take more credit for the value-added to their students' performance levels. In short, the impact that these latter institutions have on individual students is proportionately greater than that of the more exclusive institutions.

Related to the search for the best college material are the criteria of high school grades and standardized test scores, both of which have, at times, tended to reduce the educational opportunity available for those unable to cope with these yardsticks. Studies have shown that Scholastic Aptitude Test scores are subject to considerable margins of error for individuals in all groups; that students from low-income families score lower than those from families with high incomes; that women score lower than men on the computational aspects of the examination; that achievement test scores do not correlate appreciably higher with grades than scores from tests measuring other qualities; that students' scores on the Scholastic Aptitude Tests have been subject to a variety of traumas unrelated to ability; and that high school grades frequently do not correlate well with college performance. Nonetheless, admissions handicappers continue to use tests and grades and to ignore other critical human capacities that assist students in achieving success.

College grading itself has come in for severe criticism in recent years, as those who see a declining quality in standards berate faculty members for grade inflation. There is evidence that college grades bear little or no relationship to adult accomplishments or success in life. Faculty members do not adjust grades to correspond to changes in average student ability. There is some evidence that with new methods of grading, which stress student learning and mastery rather than a prescribed time limit for completion of given material, students are capable of certifying that they have achieved the learning objectives prescribed by the faculty. Nonetheless, there is still a tremendous reliance on grades earned. Although society and its institutions rely a great deal on grading systems, there is no generally accepted standard for a grade of A earned in different institutions or, for that matter, even within the same institution or the same department.

Another standard under challenge is the length of time necessary to complete a college education. People have always assumed that students completed a two-year program of study in two years, or a four-year program in four years. Recent experience, however, shows that neither of these situations always prevails. Students take longer periods of time for a variety of reasons including the acquisition of remedial skills necessary to succeed, the necessity to work, the attempt to sample courses in different programs and different institutions, and others.

With College-Level Examination Program examinations, advanced placement examinations, off-campus studies, and other practices, it is no longer even a certainty that students will spend all of their time on campus to receive a higher education. This situation may render the concept of campus meaningless.

In short, a college education has changed considerably. As James R. Davis has noted: "The boundaries which define the basic nature of a college education—its length of time, its scope of study, and its location—have become unclear."[6] It is time to devise other, more accurate measures of learning to ascertain what kind of impact the institution has made on its students.

Some new standards

How should we, then, measure quality of both individuals and institutions? Davis has noted that

> the problem is not that institutions fail to attain acceptable standards; rather, the problem is that the system *as a whole* cannot reach consensus about goals and standards. It is not that institutions of higher education are no longer pursuing standards of excellence; rather, there is honest disagreement today among institutions about ends and means.[7]

Let us look at a list of potential standards to measure quality.[8] Many of these measures can be criticized because they are not easily quantifiable, because they may not truly evaluate the attainment of the purposes of higher education, or because they may prove not to be valuable in assessing quality of education.

- degree to which institutional goals are made explicit
- attainment of long-range and annual goals
- diversity of student population profile

6. "The Search for Standards: Relativism and Emerging Pluralism in Higher Education," *Journal of Higher Education*, February 1974, p. 148.

7. Ibid.

8. Allan W. Ostar, "Quality: How is it Really Measured?", *College and University Business*, May 1973, pp. 24, 28.

- evaluation of student personnel services and extra class activities
- library book usage
- general quality of instruction
- degree of success in educating high-risk students
- students' attainment of predefined levels of achievement
- students' effective organization and use of data
- students' ability to form, understand, articulate, and apply concepts and principles from several broad areas of learning
- understanding of a particular field of knowledge
- personal qualities such as degree of motivation and enthusiasm, resourcefulness in meeting new situations, intellectual curiosity and drive
- physical and mental well-being, student satisfaction with personal goals
- ability to live and interact satisfactorily with others
- student performance in subsequent institutions, including additional degrees earned
- preparation for exployment in a particular vocation or professional area
- percentage of accepted job offers related to educational preparation
- actual student performance on the job
- active concern and/or participation in the world by graduates
- degree of public service by the college and its graduates to society
- benefits from the institution's research
- extent to which facilities are utilized efficiently and effectively by internal and external groups
- significant involvement of professional staff in community affairs
- community reaction to the institution's successes
- public awareness of philosophy and services of the college

In short, it is a "back-to-basics" movement—back to the real meaning of the basics listed in the front of the college catalog. In other words, what is to be measured is what students are actually doing and accomplishing, rather than only those things that researchers can score easily. To be sure, the measures and tests have not yet been developed for all of these, but the search is worthwhile.

Obviously, not every educational institution engages in activities related to all of the items listed. Community colleges, for instance, would have less interest in being measured on research; some four-year institutions might have less interest in preparing students for a vocation; some institutions might not care to allow their facilities to be used by the public, but might be accomplishing other public services. Each institution would list those items by which it should be measured and would analyze each year whether or not these items have been attained. The exercise of listing the standards by which it should be measured would be a healthy one inside each of the 3,000 institutions of higher learning in the United States, for it would force each college and university to focus attention, energy, and time on what its own basics are. Rather than accept externally imposed standards, institutions would be freer to describe for themselves what it is they intend to accomplish and to publicize these goals so that prospective students could measure their own objectives against those the college or university wishes to achieve.

To be sure, this plan will be criticized by some as a relativistic approach inimical to the highest needs of society. We must focus not on *the* institution of higher education but on the diverse *system* of American higher education that as a *whole* will meet those higher needs of society. Some institutions will focus more intently upon certain items and others will focus upon others. The system as a whole should meet the needs; each institution separately should meet its own objectives and at the same time some of the needs of society and of the students who come to the college's door.

For many years, we in higher education in America have been unable to define higher education. Is it the tradition of Harvard University? That institution in itself has evolved from a vocationally oriented institution to a rather diverse and comprehensive one. Is it the tradition of West Point? Or Reed College? Or any of the excellent community colleges? Obviously the strength of higher education in this nation has been its diversity. There has been no single, set pattern. There has been no one set of standards, of quality that can be measured by anyone.

Our increasingly consumer-conscious society has recently produced a spate of legal actions by individuals claiming to have been mislead or even cheated by colleges. If colleges and universities were more honest with the public (and with themselves), secondary school authorities would know what each institution intends to accomplish and could provide such colleges and universities with a profile of the students' achievements, not solely in the academic areas, but in the less tangible leadership and activity areas. This information might help to make a more comfortable fit between the individual and the institution. In turn, the institutions of higher learning could furnish the high schools with profiles and records of their own graduates, so that the fit between individual and institution could be continually refined. Entrance requirements, then, would be somewhat more meaningful in terms of the individual, rather than in terms of a norm for large numbers of individuals. The measurement, of course, is less simple; the outcome would be worth the effort.

Instead of continuing to decry the lack of standards and the demise of quality, colleges and universities would themselves be responsible for establishing the standards and levels of quality they wished to attain. To do so requires a hard look at themselves, perhaps a painful examination, but a more meaningful one.

What Standard for Equal Opportunity?

LISLE C. CARTER, JR.

In some respects the question of standards is in the eye of the beholder. It was not very long ago that some institutions practiced what Clark Kerr called "the guild approach," with virtually open admissions for most of those who were able to pay but a lamentable discrimination against students from some population groups. "Bonehead" English was not an invention of the 1960s and 1970s but of those times. And the "gentleman's C" was succinctly descriptive of the class, effort, and proficiency of particular students. Presumably standards remained intact during that earlier period, however much the admission practices of some quality institutions were to be deplored.

Many public institutions, founded as explicit alternatives to these selective schools, practiced an open door policy, under which students could enter for little or no tuition. For this reason and because they offered some peculiar, useful courses, they tended to be looked down upon by their private counterparts.

There were, of course, during that earlier period, private institutions, for example, those in large cities, that served a more diverse public as well. Historically, black colleges in particular provided a valuable service to a number of white institutions, for which they were not compensated, by relieving the latter, in good part, of an awkward problem that they were not on the whole ready to face. These institutions, with very limited resources, managed nonetheless to send presumably less qualified students on to graduate and professional studies in major public institutions. These standards of selectivity are essentially market-determined with little redeeming academic or social value.

Much else has changed, of course. Public institutions have become selective to highly selective. Private institutions receive substantial amounts of public support and are seeking more. Many private institutions are searching for students. Others are being absorbed by state systems. While private junior colleges are disappearing, public community and junior colleges are flourishing. Because law and social change have pressed public and private institutions to admit significant numbers of minority students, public and private black institutions are being required to justify their existence. Access to a college education for any person who can benefit from one has become a proposition that is broadly subscribed to. Indeed, through the 1960s and into the early 1970s, universal higher education seemed to be little more than a generation away.

Substituting new programs for existing ones

The turbulence of the campuses and the cities, disappointment in the ability of universities to solve social and economic problems, and doubts about the added economic value of higher education have contributed to a growing pessimism about the desirability or certainty of universal higher education. By far the greatest contribution to that pessimism has been the rising costs of higher education to both students and taxpayers. Concerns about standards have escalated as some of the consequences of rising costs have become more apparent. In the late 1960s, although there were some danger signs, it was still possible for many in the academic community to share the faculty view that the price for allowing professors to pursue their own priorities was broader access to the university. Unquestionably, many faculty members wholeheartedly supported special admission programs, but it is likely that others were cynical in their acquiescence.

When the financial crunch made clear that change would have to take place by substitution of new programs for some existing ones rather than by increment, claims of quality and academic standards were used to rationalize the curtailing of special scholarship assistance, supportive services, and other such frills. Budgetary constraints were used to exclude those likely to require more professorial attention. Selectivity often means absurd admissions standards that require combined Scholastic Aptitude Test score averages in excess of 1300 to enter college or a grade point average of 3.8 for admission to medical school.

Cost-conscious legislators, college and university contributors, and middle-class parents have also raised questions about expenditures to increase opportunities for higher education among disadvantaged students. Thus far, few have articulated a retreat from commitment to access for all who can benefit, but there has perhaps been a shift toward a narrower view of who can benefit. It should be plain, however, that the issue is not so much one of quality and standards as it is of costs. The student who can pay still has open access, although not necessarily at the institution of his or her choice. Rising tuition costs often prevent poor but able students from continuing their education, obstacles to providing academic support to help students from impoverished educational backgrounds. Short-term costs are thus tending to outweigh long-range benefits to society.

Nevertheless, we have come too far in our commitment to universal higher education to turn back now. About 60 percent of high school graduates pursue postsecondary education of some kind at some point in their careers. The historic role of higher education in providing credentials for any vocation has expanded to such a degree that one is more and more subject to penalty without a postsecondary degree. The problems of academic standards and student performance are real and important, but it is essential to separate these problems from higher education's response to financial stringency. Otherwise, the burden of competition for resources and fiscal retrenchment will continue to fall most heavily on particular population groups. It is not really probable that persons from upper-income families are six times more likely to benefit from a college education than persons from low-income families. "Life is unfair" is a consolation of the comfortable. A society that espouses our values should not rest easily with that axiom so long as it is capable of doing something about it.

The avenue to universal access

The nub of the issue of universal access is the question of who is worthwhile educating beyond the twelfth grade and to what level beyond. That question cannot be answered in advance. Even among persons with similar backgrounds, it is not easy to know who will make the best use of a college education. Although Scholastic Aptitude Tests apparently do a reasonably good job of predicting initial success in academic coursework, they certainly provide no help in predicting success in career or life. They neither take into account nor allow for differences in economic, cultural, or social backgrounds; nor can they measure motivation, creativity, persuasiveness, or the ability to persist.

One important response to this dilemma is to use the community college as the avenue of universal postsecondary access. Growth in enrollment in these institutions has far surpassed growth in four-year institutions. Community colleges have provided a valuable service in offering technical training and specialized education for a wide range of occupations; they have also been important vehicles for continuing education programs. They have, however, been less useful as means of access to bachelors' degrees. It can be argued, of course, that this demonstrates that those who go to community colleges for academic work have not the intellectual capacity to acquire the degree. But evidence suggests that the students of similar backgrounds who go to four-year institutions initially are more likely to complete a four-year program than those who enter through the community college. Too often the two-year institution has been used by the four-year institution to avoid its responsibilities.

Whatever the means of entry, the pursuit of learning and demonstrable proficiency should be the goals of institutions for their students. Neither of those goals is likely to be attained without substantial commitment and effort.

Alexander Astin, a leading analyst of higher education data, reminded us recently that the best chances for success are to be found in small residential institutions, while the large nonresidential urban institutions offer the poorest chances. These findings give strong and concrete support to the continued importance and value of private and public historically black colleges and other small residential institutions that serve a diverse clientele; they also point up the special problems faced by the four-year and two-year urban institutions that undertake to provide broad access to students. It is hard for the latter institutions to provide the special attention, the supportive environment, and the institutional attachment that seem closely linked to successful student performance. Yet these are the institutions that are expected to bear the principal burden in assuming equality of opportunity for higher education. Clearly, this is a reasonable proposition only if society is prepared to devote more resources to programs likely to make that opportunity real.

The following suggest some essential characteristics of such programs without attempting to be definitive or specific:

1. There should be increased exploration of periodic proficiency measures in reading comprehension, writing, and computational skills, not as exclusionary or ranking devices, but as a means of diagnostic assistance to advisors, counselors, and students. It is essential that such measures be linked to systematic and readily available developmental programs to help students overcome any deficiencies.

2. Faculty members should teach in ways that recognize that, in urban institutions, the instructional programs are the only assured chance to engage the students' interest and attachment.

3. The academic program should be flexible enough to accommodate students stopping in and out of the institution and to accommodate different scheduling needs based on a variety of job and family circumstances. Programs should also have enough flexibility to allow students to advance at their own speed in meeting academic requirements.

4. Supportive services should be provided to help students with problems they encounter outside the institutional setting as well as within it.

5. Neither supportive services, innovative instruction, nor flexible programs should be seen as implying less than rigorous content. Students who do show particular aptitude should be offered a variety of incentives to keep them challenged and involved with academic work.

None of these suggestions would benefit disadvantaged students alone, but would serve generally to enhance our urban institutions;

all of the suggestions would cost money. Moreover, they would probably have to be in place for a sustained period of time to show substantial results. Why in these circumstances should society or higher education undertake them?

The answer for society is relatively straightforward. Despite some contentions to the contrary, there is still evidence that education pays off in economic terms for both society and for persons from low-income groups, minorities, and women. Moreover, in a democracy the gains of a better educated citizenry are not to be dismissed lightly.

But is the university not being asked to do too much, to make up for the deficits of public education, of the family, perhaps of society as a whole, to function as a social service rather than as an educational institution? The unique comprehensive and accessible character of higher education in the United States, which stems from the beginning of the land grant college more than 100 years ago, has now become the responsibility of the whole higher education establishment. Not that every institution needs to play the same role, but each must play some part. The prestigious private universities, four-year institutions, and the flagship public institutions must examine their own admissions standards to give weight in some substantial and continuing way to characteristics of disadvantage such as poverty, poor educational background, culture, and race. They should pursue research as to how best to do this, but in the meantime, they must be courageous enough to exercise judgment. It is of paramount importance that these institutions enter into supportive partnerships with the two-year institutions in their respective states toward the end of assuring that there is a clear articulation between the content and competence of academic programs at two-year institutions and at four-year institutions. This in turn would assure that two-year graduates have a genuine opportunity to progress through four-year institutions if they choose to do so.

In the end, the standard for equal opportunity should be the same as the standard for all enterprises in higher education. That is, does higher education demonstrate excellence in the pursuit of its particular mission? In the case of equal opportunity, does it give the student who genuinely wants a higher education a real chance to achieve one?

What Will the Future Bring?

DAVID P. GARDNER

LIFELONG LEARNING—or, if one prefers, further education or recurrent education—while not a concept of recent origin, is at present effecting significant changes in higher education, both in this country and abroad. These changes carry with them the possibility of a more enduring and intimate relation than has heretofore existed between the recurring educational needs of people throughout their lives and the character and mission of the institutions serving them. Indeed, such changes can, in some cases, be expected to alter institutions in kind and not in just the degree of their involvement in further education programs. In addition, new institutions, public and private, will be created both within and outside of the traditional academic community.

In this country, the challenge of lifelong learning was long ago accepted, as is evidenced by the well-established continuing education and extension programs of our colleges and universities. In examining afresh the potential for further education programs, one tends to overlook the richness and variety of experiences and experiments that have defined these programs over the years. These established efforts should be more systematically assessed, not only to discover how best to expand what is now being offered, but also to make whatever changes may be required now and in the future.

The time is propitious for giving effort and thought to lifelong learning: Better a knowing and deliberate adaptation to social and educational change than a belated and stumbling response or halfhearted accommodation. In 1974, Ernest L. Boyer warned that we should not project on the future outworn assumptions from the past, nor should we permit our preoccupation with retrenchment and the steady state to place a cap on both our spirit and our sense of the future.[1] "Hardly anywhere," as W. R. Niblett has observed, "is it generally believed that the recipe for meeting the next twenty years is to continue to do, only better, what has been done in the last twenty."[2] Thus, the single-valued forecasts and perspectives which dominated academic planning and expansion in the 1960s ought not to limit the present range of policy options or to compromise promising alternative strategies for integrating lifelong learning programs and initiatives with the more established and familiar forms of higher education.[3]

The opportunities of change

The industrially advanced countries of the world are undergoing important social changes that ought surely to engage educators in more reflective and analytical thinking about lifelong learning than they are ordinarily accustomed to. Various knowledgeable observers, including the Carnegie Commission on Higher Education, anticipate such changes as progressive reduction in the work week, accompanied by an increase in real hourly income; expansion of the service sector of the economy, with its more flexible working schedule; and a rising rate of urbanization, accompanied by changes in life styles and values that demand a more varied and enriching pattern of life experiences and militate against rigid and harsh working conditions.

The opportunities for higher education presented by these changes are as substantial as the problems arising from them are formidable. They can perhaps best be phrased as problems for consideration. Higher education will be afforded the chance to think anew about

- the relation between work and study
- the assumptions underlying the space and time conditions of instruction
- curricula and educational policies rooted in articulation arrangements now existing among institutions and in assumptions about the continuity of enrollment that will probably be less valid in the future than they have been in the past

1. "Breaking Up the Youth Ghetto," in *Lifelong Learners: A New Clientele for Higher Education,* ed. Dyckman W. Vermilye, Current Issues in Higher Education (San Francisco: Jossey-Bass, 1974), p. 5.

2. "Issues and Choices," in *Universities Facing the Future,* ed. W. R. Niblett and R. F. Butts (San Francisco: Jossey-Bass, 1972), p. 3.

3. See David P. Gardner, "Forces for Change in American Higher Education," in *On the Meaning of the University,* ed. Sterling M. McMurrin (Salt Lake City: University of Utah Press, 1976), pp. 103–23.

CARL A. RUDISILL LIBRARY
LENOIR RHYNE COLLEGE

• the effect that a greater mix of age groups on campus will have on student subcultures, the learning environment, and administrative arrangements
• the need for programs of faculty development that both anticipate and provide the means for dealing with the new and unfamiliar demands made by older students as well as those of traditional college-age students.

Although this list is not inclusive, it at least illustrates some of the issues with which higher education must contend. It is to be hoped that our colleges and universities will cope with these demands in the same spirit as in the past they handled other demands: as when the self-contained classical college came to terms with the land-grant movement following the Civil War; and when the modern university and college responded to the national call for a move from a limited to a mass system of higher education following World War II.

Such accommodation is already taking place in typically pluralistic fashion. Not only have well-established continuing education programs responded in their own ways to freshly perceived opportunities, but also major new programs have been launched in New York, Minnesota, Nebraska, Florida, and California, among other states.[4] Other such programs will follow as people make lifelong-learning demands on our institutions and as colleges and universities, in turn, adapt their capabilities and purposes to the fulfillment of their broader social and educational obligations.

Of the many issues associated with the lifelong learning movement today, two areas of special concern have less often been the objects of attention than their importance warrants: the need for more intensive discussion among all sectors of society, and the probable impact on the educational policies of academic institutions.

Widening the discussion

Although some communication has been initiated between the higher education institution on the one hand and representatives of labor, business, government (at all levels), and other major social institutions and organizations on the other, the kind of discussion I

4. For an informative study of sixteen such programs, see Leland Medsker, Stewart Edelstein, Hannah Kreplin, Janet Ruyle, and John Shea, *Extending Opportunities for a College Degree: Practices, Problems, and Potentials* (Berkeley, Calif.: Center for Research and Development in Higher Education, 1975).

am proposing has not yet taken place in this country as it has, for example, in Sweden and France. Our colleges and universities have tended to be concerned principally with the financial and structural implications of the movement for themselves, and they have calculated their initiatives and their responses accordingly. However understandable that is from an institutional (or, more precisely, from an administrative) point of view, such a limited outlook produces responses that are narrow, self-serving, and unlikely to yield the inclusive and sustainable results we should be seeking. More exchange of views is needed, and perhaps the American Council—alone or in concert with other higher education associations—could find the most useful and least cumbersome ways to open up such conversations, just as policy-makers at the state level might initiate discussions as circumstances best suggest.

The inclusion of educational entitlements in fringe-benefit collective bargaining contracts is common now in Sweden, is becoming more frequent in other industrially advanced nations, and is inching its way into labor-management discussions in our own country. Many states now require that practicing professionals take continuing education courses for recertification and relicensing, and many more states will probably soon impose such legal requirements. Similarly, private organizations and public agencies alike are coming to recognize that their managerial and professional cadres need periodically to refurbish and update their skills. The nation's institutions are, in short, gradually becoming aware that, for societies as complex, sophisticated, and competitive as our own, the idea "that full-time education should be digested all in one gulp, from age 5 to 22," as Lord Eric Ashby puts it, is untenable.[5] A wiser course might be to encourage the enrollment of highly motivated adult students in higher education and at the same time to reduce the enrollment of marginally committed younger students, whose presence now tends to weaken the overall effectiveness of our colleges and universities.

In any event, the changing nature of the job market may prove to be the overriding variable, should the period of time spent in formal education during early life diminish, while the periods available later for study expand. Thus, the need for the higher education community to seek out and take into account the perceptions of labor, business,

5. *Any Person, Any Study: An Essay of Higher Education in the United States* (New York: McGraw-Hill, 1971), p. 99.

and public service representatives ought to be as self-evident and self-generating as the reverse: the need for business, labor, and public service to plan for recurrent education.

Calculating the effect

My second concern is with the impact, whether intended or inadvertent, of the lifelong learning movement on the educational policies and practices of academic institutions, as distinguished from the financial and structural implications, which ordinarily are the first considered.

In their sixteen-case study of extended degree programs (one very important aspect of the overall movement), Medsker and his colleagues paid particular attention to this issue. As the study noted, some programs were intended to have no direct effect (or even indirect, for that matter) on established institutional policies and practices—they were to be stand-alone efforts—whereas others were deliberately intended to bring about major academic changes (or reforms, if one prefers) in conventional educational programs as well as in the financial and governing structures of the institutions. Medsker concludes:

> Our study has given us cause for concern about expressed intentions to assign the task of academic reform to programs destined to meet the needs of special students. It seems clear that many administrators, legislators, and others interested in campus reform view extended degree programs as instruments for achieving needed changes in higher education. It is interesting to note that in discussing the potential for academic reform, staff in programs housed in existing institutions and those in newly created institutions tended to share a common anxiety: that there was more likelihood of on-campus conventional programs coming to have a constraining effect on extended degree programs than that extended degree programs would influence the traditional ones. Actually, changes will doubtless take place in both directions, and mutual impact is probably inevitable.[6]

What Medsker's observations suggest is that an evolutionary, incremental kind of change is most likely to occur but that change is inevitable. If this prediction proves true, then higher education in this decade and certainly into the next can be expected to assimilate, or at least to accommodate, a variety of alternative, unconventional, and nontraditional programs and practices.

The responses of institutions to lifelong learning will not be homogeneous, nor should they be. The degree of change—to be welcomed

6. *Extending Opportunities for a College Degree*, p. 293.

or endured, depending on one's point of view—will vary enormously: at one extreme, a virtual transformation of programs and institutions; at the other, a mere tinkering with admissions policies to ease somewhat the entry of part-time older students. But impact there will surely be on higher education as a whole. Thus, it may be best for institutions of higher education to consider more carefully than they so far have what place in the scheme of things they wish eventually to hold. In short, a more inclusive and extended analysis of institutional options and opportunities is needed, an analysis that reaches beyond considerations of how lifelong learning programs will affect enrollments in the next biennium or will disturb the administrative turf on campus at any given time.

A view of the future

Despite some bold utterances and actual initiatives undertaken in some states, the lifelong learning movement is still very much in its formative stages. That there exists at present no overall plan, or even a consensus about the future course of the movement, is probably just as well; certainly it is in keeping with the highly decentralized and pluralistic character of American higher education. The pattern of institutional response is likely to emerge over time out of a patchwork of ideas and programs tried and tested: What proves out will be retained, and what does not will be discarded or revised anew.

The anticipation of such a gradual and evolutionary development of the lifelong learning idea should not, however, excuse policy-makers from thinking hard about the future. The lifelong learning movement calls for nothing less than the most careful analysis possible of fundamental questions about the purposes of higher education as they bear upon both the students to be served and the institutions serving them. As Ashby observes:

> Colleges and universities, like libraries and museums, may come to be places which receive students throughout life, not only as adolescents from school. They may withdraw from any deliberate program of induction for the passage from adolescence to adulthood, on the ground that the norms of behaviour and opinion which society requires of its initiates are in flux, and the old norms are outdated. Institutions of higher education may restrict their educational function to cultivating one way—recognizing that it is not the only—of reaching conclusions about man, society, and nature. A college degree, like a passport, may have to be renewed by examination every few years if it is to remain valid. A policy on these lines would leave systems of higher

education free to devote themselves to the functions they are competent to discharge. It would simplify treatment of the question: what should be taught?[7]

Indeed, it is not unreasonable to speculate that, by the turn of the century, many of our campuses will be transformed from centers of learning into learning centers that house a highly mobile population of students and scholars, a small resident population studying primarily at the most advanced levels (and by the very ablest students at all levels), and an integrated network of libraries, computers, television, and other teaching resources designed as much for residential as for off-campus study and research; in short, the campus will have become a network of associations, arrangements, and resources that will permit students to have the university or college with them at home, at work, and at leisure throughout their lifetimes.[8]

However imprecise these speculations may prove to be, there is no doubt that the nation's colleges and universities will in the coming years be questioning with greater intensity many of the current assumptions about *who* will partake of their programs, and *how, when,* and *where* they will do so. Both students and their institutions are implicated in the answers to these questions. The process of arriving at answers will be helped along by our anticipating the challenge of lifelong learning in our own thoughts and in the discharge of our institutional responsibilities.

The Alchemy of Lifelong Learning

SUSAN RINK, B.V.M.

USING A MEDICAL METAPHOR, one might compare the concept of lifelong learning to a virus that has not only infected individuals but has spread to what may be epidemic proportions. Carriers of the virus are everywhere; instead of being considered hazardous and kept in isolation, they should be encouraged to make contact with as many other people as possible. Because the infection has no chronological or geographical limits, it presents the delightful danger of becoming pandemic.

7. *Any Person, Any Study,* pp. 100–101.
8. See "Forces for Change in American Higher Education."

Interest in lifelong learning is rampant, among academicians, politicians, gerontologists, corporation presidents, union leaders. But along with that interest go a host of urgent questions: What is the academic quality of these new types of students? What are their interests? What problems of access will they have at different stages in the lifelong learning span? What will traditional faculty think about these new learners? What will the new learners think about the faculty? What administrative problems will arise? In short, what must post-secondary educators anticipate as they face the challenge of lifelong learning?

Mundelein College anticipated twelve years ago and has collected considerable data that may help answer these questions. Before reporting these data, I believe a few general remarks may be helpful.

The term *lifelong learning* means different things to different people, but I share the broad view of those who see it "as an opportunity to improve the mix and change the traditional sequence of education, work and leisure."[1] Those who hold this view must accept the full meaning of universal postsecondary education; they must be willing to deal with minorities, men and women, adult and traditional-age students.

The concept of lifelong learning carries with it many problems that must be solved. Institutions seriously considering the concept soon realize that their educational missions as well as their resources may limit their ability to implement even one successful program. To the small liberal arts college that has long been recognized for its high-quality teaching, responsive curriculum, and close teacher-student relations—a college that has perhaps built a reputation for excellence in a few areas—new learners can be a threat. The challenge—in addition to meeting the needs of new publics or changing the mix of education, work, and leisure—is "to find new programs or services that will add distinctiveness to the school. This is called positioning—finding a viable niche in the market."[2] If more than short-term success is to be achieved, the new niche must fit closely with the college's established mission. But even with a close fit, tremendous changes at every level

1. *The Lifelong Learning Act and Options for a Federal Lifelong Learning Policy, Title I, Part B, P.L. 94-482.* A Policy/Options Statement by the Education Policy Committee of the Association of Colleges and Schools of Education in State Universities and Land-Grant Colleges and Affiliated Private Universities, and the Government Relations Commission of the American Association of Colleges for Teacher Education (Washington: 1977).

2. Nancy Harper, in an interview with Philip Kotler, "Why We Need Marketing," *Currents,* May 1977, p. 8.

of administration, faculty, and staff will be required to prevent the new program's becoming just one more ephemeral experiment or stop-gap measure to combat declining enrollments.

The Mundelein experience

Mundelein College has seven nontraditional programs that incorporate the concept of lifelong learning. The success of these programs can be attributed to a faculty that prides itself on being true to the college's mission and maintaining academic standards while at the same time creating new opportunities for learning.

The focus of this paper is on the Weekend College in Residence (WEC), on its students, and on the many changes necessary to make this program an integral part of the college. Launched in 1974, the program was designed to serve one segment of the lifelong learning population: the fully employed adult student who is unable or unwilling to attend night classes. In its three years of existence, WEC has grown considerably: from 9.3 percent of our total student enrollment in the fall of 1974 to about 40 percent in the fall of 1977. (In full-time-equivalent figures, the increase was from 8.8 percent to 37 percent.)[3]

Historically, Mundelein had already had some experience serving adults, having in 1965 positioned itself to provide for the education of adult women. But a weekday program for commuting women posed few administrative problems compared with a weekend program for commuting and resident men and women ranging in age from nineteen to seventy. Mixing education with work and leisure and holding weekend classes for employed adults meant changing to a seven-day operation; other changes affecting the institution as a whole are discussed later.

The findings presented here come from eight months of intensive research on the WEC.[4] These data are reported in three main categories: academic quality, attrition, and faculty and student perceptions.

3. Data from a demographic study by Jacqueline L. Cuevas, a WEC psychology major.

4. This research was funded as part of an Advanced Institutional Development Program grant (under Title III of the Higher Education Act of 1965). Except for the demographic study, the remaining research was done for the College by Ronald Cervero, a Ph.D. candidate from the University of Chicago. All data were supplied by Tina Stretch, Director of the Weekend College, and were analyzed using the Statistical Package for the Social Sciences at the University of Chicago Computation Center. The results of the research were presented in five separate papers from March to August 1977.

Academic quality

One study of 160 students—all of whom had completed twenty-one semester hours of regular college course work before entering the Weekend College and had completed at least twenty-one semester hours of course work in the WEC—found that their grade-point average as WEC students was 2.08 on a three-point scale, whereas their GPA for regular course work had been 1.61. This difference of almost half a grade point was highly significant statistically. Other data seem to indicate that the higher GPA was not due simply to grade inflation. A possible interpretation is that, by the time they enroll in WEC, these students have become more mature, more goal-directed, and more highly motivated.

Grades given to weekend students did not differ significantly from those given to weekday students taking identical courses taught by the same or by different instructors. Weekend students were consistently more likely than weekday students to take "Incompletes" in courses; in the fall of 1976, 7.9 percent of the weekend course registrations, compared with 3.8 percent of the weekday course registrations, resulted in Incompletes. There is little likelihood that these courses will ever actually be completed by students.

The type of course taken was a significant factor in the proportion of Incompletes given, the difference being most pronounced between quantitative and reflective courses. Only about 1 percent of the students in quantitative courses, but 16 percent of those in reflective courses, did not complete their course work during the term. The most reasonable explanation is that students in quantitative courses are given more precise assignments, are evaluated more frequently, and can more readily integrate this type of knowledge into their busy lives. Students in reflective courses tend to want additional time and leisure to assimilate their new learning.

For a population of 277 students, the average length of time out of school before returning to enroll in the Weekend College was 6.9 years; the range was from one year to forty years. The student's performance was not related to the number of years out of school. Moreover, the correlation between age and GPA was only .12, and the direction of the correlation indicated that, if anything, GPAs increase as students get older. Data such as these should certainly be used in counseling adults who may be reluctant to return to school because they fear competition with younger students.

Attrition

Accurate attrition studies are difficult to carry out in the context of lifelong learning since most such studies assume that a college education takes four years. Obviously, such an assumption will not work when one is dealing with a highly mobile student population that may be returning to continue or complete postsecondary education after a period of years out of school. Yet administrators who must plan systematically and who recognize the positive correlation between student retention and institutional survival must be concerned with attrition. Therefore, the attrition studies conducted with WEC students had two purposes: to formulate a definition of attrition appropriate for non-traditional students and to ascertain why students withdraw from the Weekend College.

Three samples were studied. The first comprised seventy-four WEC graduates, 89 percent of whom had attended for consecutive terms. Of the remaining 11 percent, five students had missed one term, two had missed two terms, and one had missed three terms. The second sample comprised eighty currently enrolled WEC students from a random sample of 218 with completed admissions records. Of these, 85 percent had attended for consecutive terms. Of the remaining 15 percent, nine subjects had missed one term, and the other three had missed two terms. The third sample consisted of the 138 students from the random sample of 218 mentioned above who had not registered during the spring or fall of 1977. Of these, 72 percent had withdrawn after only one term, 25 percent after two terms, 11 percent after three terms, 7 percent after four terms, and the remaining 5 percent after five or more terms of enrollment.

Two conclusions may be drawn from these data. First, the more frequently people register for courses, the more likely they are to remain in the program. The implication for administrators is that students should be monitored closely during their first and second terms, when they are more likely to drop out. The second conclusion is that the student who fails to register for the next term is not likely to register again, and the student who does not register for two consecutive terms may be considered an attrition statistic. It follows that, to the extent students can be encouraged to enroll in consecutive terms, the WEC retention rate can be increased.

The seventy-one students who withdrew gave various reasons (they were allowed to indicate more than one): 53 percent cited academic reasons; 29 percent, employment; 51 percent, financial problems; and 49 percent, personal reasons.

Faculty and student perceptions of WEC

In June 1977, key faculty members and administrators met at a week-long workshop to make decisions on the WEC curriculum. In preparation for the workshop, fifty-three faculty members who taught in WEC during the winter 1977 term were asked to complete a survey on their perceptions of the Weekend College, its curriculum, and its students; forty completed the survey, for a 76 percent response rate. These faculty members averaged ten years in college-level teaching and had taught an average of 4.5 courses in the WEC. In addition, student perceptions were solicited prior to the workshop; the population for the study was 483 students.

The responses of faculty and students may be summarized as follows:

• According to faculty, WEC students were similar to other students in motivation and class participation; they were also perceived as being prepared for class, grade-conscious, and able to work well on their own.

• About two-thirds of the faculty believed that the level of learning in the WEC was comparable to that observed in other teaching situations.

• According to faculty, WEC students did not expect—and should not receive—special consideration because of the many outside pressures on their lives.

• Faculty members thought that most WEC students attended classes primarily for job-related reasons. Moreover, about one in three believed that a major goal of the Weekend College is and should be job preparation. In general, students were likely to indicate that personal enjoyment and satisfaction were their major reasons for enrolling in WEC, although job- and career-related reasons were important to students in all areas of academic concentration.

• Faculty agreed with students about what learning activities took place in WEC courses. They cited as the most frequent extralearning activities student-to-teacher phone calls, extra class sessions, materials placed on reserve, student-to-student phone calls, and films.

• Two-thirds of the faculty respondents, but only one-fourth of the students respondents, thought that more classroom hours should be scheduled.

• In moving from the regular college program to the WEC, most of the instructors had to modify their course content and teaching style, but fewer than half had to redesign their courses extensively. Changes included increased reading and writing assignments, less class discussion, reduction in the amount of material covered in class, and more specificity of program objectives. (Aside from the survey, it was observed that some faculty members became less long-winded and refrained from telling their usual anecdotes in WEC classes.)

• Though the question was not asked in the survey, the Academic Dean observed that many faculty members prefer to teach students in the lifelong learning programs, especially in the WEC

• Close to half of the WEC students had lived on campus for at least a short period of time; of those, all but two mentioned the many benefits—both cognitive and affective—that being in residence added to their education.

• WEC students differed very little from one another in their ordering of the purposes of a college of education. Among the most important to them were development of the ability to think, to read, and to write. Rated low were development of the ability to appreciate the arts and to understand the world in mathematical terms.

• Close to three in four WEC students said they had sought advice on course selection at least once after their initial interview by the WEC staff.

• Seven in ten WEC students said they were able to integrate their work and educational worlds while attending the WEC.

• In general, students agreed with WEC objectives in that they believed that interpersonal relationships were an important part of learning in the WEC; they sought out faculty apart from the classroom; they believed they would continue learning after graduation; they felt little pressure to compete with others; and they regarded the opinions of other students as important.

The effect and future of the WEC

This major program in lifelong learning has been gratifyingly successful. The Hawthorne Effect seems to have operated in the first year, when everything done for the first experimental group of students added to their appreciation of the program. Each successive term has revealed more examples of the massive effort required to genuinely mix the pattern of work, study, and leisure.

WEC students are charged the same tuition and offered the same quality of education as other students at Mundelein. In addition, they are provided with similar services. Nonetheless, as was mentioned earlier, making the Weekend College an integral part of the institution as a whole required some drastic changes. First, besides the faculty and staff needed for WEC, employees had to be added to the registrar's office, the business office, and the library; security guards, custodians, elevator operators, and even a lifeguard had to be hired. Second, the hours for the bookstore, counseling office, career center, and cafeteria were changed. Third, new admissions criteria for people without ACT or SAT scores or counselors' recommendations had to be established, as did new scholarship criteria and even new procedures for voting for Who's Who and class officers. Fourth, the director of the WEC was elevated to a top administrative position. Finally, a newly designed team-taught course entitled Strategies for Learning is required of most adult students.

Despite these changes, a few WEC students have said they feel like second-class citizens because some particular service, teacher, or program is not available on the weekend. But the most serious problems have come from weekday students, some of whom also say they feel like second-class citizens and who sometimes make remarks like "All the good teachers now teach on the weekends," or "Meals are better on weekends." The local media have helped to reinforce this false image in that they often prefer to feature a story about a thirty-five-year-old or fifty-year-old freshman to one about the traditional eighteen-year-old.

Being fully aware of enrollment projections, Mundelein anticipates growth in this particular lifelong learning program, but at a much slower rate than in the past. We expect more requests for advanced work on weekends. Until this year, no laboratory or language courses have been offered, but now take-home science kits are being designed, and infinite care has gone into preparing an elementary language course for weekenders. Mundelein will continue to experiment with ways to accommodate courses to a new format.

Institutions of all kinds—from small community colleges to large universities—will be called upon to respond to the challenge of lifelong learning. Perhaps the findings presented here—though they cover only a small part of the topic—will be helpful to others planning different but equally important programs of this nature.

Perhaps more appropriate than the medical metaphor with which this paper opened is a metaphor suggested by a friend of mine nearing the end of a brilliant teaching and research career. The alchemists of the Middle Ages sought the formula for transmuting ignoble metals into gold. Lifelong learning may be like the alchemical process: transforming the learning and experiences of younger years into the knowledge and wisdom of the golden years.

Motivating Business
to Support Education

JOHN T. FEY

IT IS NOT THE PURPOSE OF THIS PAPER TO BELABOR the obvious: It should be abundantly clear that corporations have a substantial stake in higher education. Is there anyone in business who has not benefited personally in some way from college or graduate studies? Or even more to the point, where would businesses be today without the marvels of technology, the advances in science, medicine, and the arts that so often owe their origins to the training and research that take place in the great academic institutions?

No one seriously questions the vital connection between business and education—the good, hard economic reality of the benefits that flow from our centers of higher learning to the world of commerce and industry. It is a concept akin to motherhood. But if the relationship is examined somewhat more closely, it becomes apparent that there is a good deal more than just interest in the bottom line that should motivate business to accept the importance of its obligation to support higher education.

Before getting into that, however, let us take a look at some of the problems facing colleges and universities in recent years.

Financial problems

It may be understating the case to say that the world of public and private higher learning is in deep financial trouble. The much-heralded Carnegie Study, released in 1970, only confirmed what many in higher education already knew too well: The undercapitalized expansion and rapid growth of the early 1960s, coupled with a slowdown in student enrollment and constantly rising costs, conspired to create fiscal crisis in many an overextended institution.

115

Tuition, which covers only 17 percent of costs in public institutions and 59 percent in private institutions, has had to go up, leaving many worthy aspirants, unable to scratch up the money, out in the cold. Even an acceptable rise in tuition has been no match for the increasing financial burden of the institutions. Just by way of illustration, over the five-year period 1972–1977, the average annual tuition charges at private colleges and universities went up more than $1,100, a rate between 2 percent and 6 percent *higher* than the Consumer Price Index advance over the same period. This trend continues with no sign of abatement.

Colleges, which had become accustomed to their liberally funded research activities, community and public services, and generous scholarship programs, rather abruptly have found themselves short of the means to sustain these activities at prior levels. The cost of graduate education, already high (especially in the case of medical education), has continued to drift even higher. A rough estimate currently puts medical school tuition expenses at about $40,000 for a four-year course at a private school.

Demographic forces and uncertainties of funding have been cause for increasing worry. The changing patterns of enrollment and continuity of the student population have complicated the task of college planners, who have been hard pressed to predict program needs. Similarly, the shifts in public attitudes and emphasis, which bear directly on what the college can or should provide, have added to the problem of planning and forecasting. Illustrative of such recent developments are increasing demand for adult education; a heavier emphasis on opening up careers for women; shifts in favored educational specialties; greater focusing on remedial measures to correct inadequacies in secondary school preparation; expanding interest in training for second careers.

As a backdrop to these difficulties and uncertainties, we find perhaps a touch of disenchantment in the public mood—an erosion in the popular faith in the power of education to improve society, to reduce income inequality, and to break down social stratification. The heavy educational expenditures by government during the heyday of the Great Society have been viewed by some as having had little beneficial effect on the performance of students (as exemplified by declining standardized test scores), their rather bad behavior during the 1960s, and the relative social position and salary advantages of college graduates. In short, the great progress toward a more just and fulfilled society that education was supposed to activate never really came to pass. Never mind that this may have been too much to lay on education's doorstep in the first place. The voters, with some justification, felt that they had been shortchanged, and education has consequently come to occupy something less than its former exalted status on the legislative appropriations agenda as well as in the minds and hearts of those who would be its beneficiaries.

The crisis in private institutions

To a greater or lesser extent, these uncertainties and hard realities have plagued all our institutions of higher learning, both public and private. The brunt, however, has generally been borne by the private institutions, which must depend on tuition, gifts, and endowments for 85 percent of their income, in contrast to public colleges, which derive 80 percent of their income from federal, state, and local governments.[1]

J. Peter Williamson cites some sobering statistics on closings of colleges.[2] Before 1967, there were few closings; then the number rose rapidly, reaching a high of forty-four in 1971–72. Lately, the rate of closings has dropped dramatically, but during the crunch most of the institutions closing down were private. Economic reversals and the stock market decline of recent years have had a deleterious effect on the private schools, whose income and investment results have been correspondingly depressed. The tuition gap between public and private colleges has also been regarded as one of the central factors involved in the rapid decline of the private colleges. Private tuition averages from three to five times the tuition for public four-year colleges and universities, and the difference is growing. The result, of course, has been to diminish severely the share of total enrollment held by private institutions. Some of the more pessimistic forecasters have suggested that continuance of current trends may soon cause private education to price itself right out of the market.

Most everyone would agree that such a result cannot be permitted to occur. But, before uncritically concluding that such a result is unacceptable, let us examine first, whether the value of private

1. Carnegie Commission on Higher Education, *Higher Education: Who Pays? Who Benefits? Who Should Pay?* (Washington, D.C.: 1973).

2. J. Peter Williamson, ed., *Funds for the Future* (New York: McGraw-Hill, 1975), p. 25.

higher education continues to justify its existence; and second, why business should have a concern.

According to Williamson, every recent study of higher education has endorsed the importance of private higher education. For instance, the 1973 Report of the National Commission on the Financing of Postsecondary Education identified three objectives for higher education that are well served by private institutions. The first is student access.

> Each individual should be able to enroll in some form of postsecondary education appropriate to that person's needs, capability and motivation.

The second objective sounds an even clearer call for private institutions.

> Postsecondary education should offer programs of formal instruction and other learning opportunities and engage in research and public service of sufficient diversity to be responsive to the changing needs of individuals and society.

The National Commission included institutional independence as the third special value of private education:

> Institutions of postsecondary education should have sufficient freedom and flexibility to maintain institutional and professional integrity and to meet creatively and responsibly their educational goals.[3]

Both public and private institutions are subject to pressures, some good and some bad, from outside and from inside. But the pressures differ, and the dissimilarities assure the distinctive contribution of private institutions to higher education.

If private institutions are to provide a variety of choice, diversity, and institutional independence, it is obvious that they must be financially secure and not overdependent on revenues from any one source. This goal would not be easy to achieve even in good times; but in a period when the financial prospects for all higher education seem so uncertain and the temptation to turn to government sources of revenues so great, it becomes even more difficult.

Let there be no misunderstanding about business's concern with the difficulties facing *publicly* funded higher education. Both public and private schools are financially troubled. Both contribute to a system in which the widest possible choices are available for students.

3. Ibid.

The influence of private institutions enriches all education, and our society—the world in which we do business—can ill afford the decline or extinction of either element in this uniquely productive dual system.

Business concern

Why should business be concerned? What is its stake? We have already seen that there is an obvious "bottom line" stake. As Milton Eisenhower of Johns Hopkins University once said: "Higher education and business are basically interdependent. One needs money to produce educated people, and the other needs educated people to produce money."

Notwithstanding the skeptics, economic studies time and again have confirmed the role of higher education in the growth of individuals and the nation. Brookings scholar Edward F. Denison has produced some landmark studies in the past decade and a half that convincingly identify the respective contributions of education in the labor force and university research toward national economic growth.

Business obviously has great need for skilled persons in the work force, and these persons are recruited from colleges and universities. Business also has a great need to develop improved communication and understanding between colleges and itself. It is important that colleges understand the economic basis of business. The corporate charter is granted at the pleasure of the legislature and the people. If business is to operate successfully—indeed, even to exist—it must justify itself in the eyes of the public. Business therefore needs the understanding and support of institutions and their graduates.

While we could play up this self-interest connection for all it's worth, there are plenty of other reasons for fostering continued and increased corporate support of higher education. The educational stake of business cannot be measured in profits alone. The state of our society provides perhaps an even more compelling reason. The major social problems—be they urban decay, crime, poverty, or equality—are too huge for any sector of our society to solve alone. Government alone cannot do it, as the programs of the 1960s have proved. The private sector cannot handle it; some things are simply beyond the competence and resources of business. What is needed is the joint support of business, government, and educational institutions, working together toward common solution of the social ills that afflict us. This is a big package, and novel approaches are being designed by such outstanding institutions as Columbia University, Wharton School of Finance and Commerce, and Stanford University. We in business should support and cooperate with these efforts in a partnership that brings into play the powers of government, the wealth and talents of business, and the sophisticated research and planning of our institutions of higher education.

Finally, although I have concentrated rather heavily on what education can do for business, we should not ignore the other side of the coin. After all, it is one thing to give but quite another to specify how the gifts should be used. I would hope that in business's support of education, due respect is accorded the absolute necessity of educational integrity and independence.

Schools must be permitted to maintain a certain autonomy even in the face of the current financial crisis. In the long run it is counter-productive to bend curriculum or otherwise shape educational purposes in terms of business needs. The history of support reflects this and there is no reason to expect that this will change. At times there are great temptations for business to externalize its costs—of training, research; of allocating people to work roles; of testing, licensing—to the university. This should not be allowed; it is expensive for the university and can pervert its aims.

We have noted that business needs the understanding of the educational community, that a greater degree of communication between the two is needed. But communication is a two-way street, and business must also understand the value of liberal education—or any education. In contrast with the rather limited purposes of business, the purposes of education are manifold and deserve support regardless of whether they are consistent with business objectives or are understood by business leaders. Mind you, this is not an endorsement of campus anarchy or educational irresponsibility, but merely an appeal for a special appreciation of the value of educational independence and of the goods that arise from it, which are not readily measured by traditional economic standards.

What business can do

Most critical and immediate, of course, are the financial needs of higher education. Studies show that business contributions to education have been on the increase, but as a proportion of pre-tax net earnings, the track record could be better. According to the joint survey of

1975 contributions by the Conference Board and the Council for Financial Aid to Education, corporate contributions to all categories of beneficiaries totaled slightly less than the year previous (which probably reflects the profit decline for the period), and education received virtually the same portion of the gift dollar in 1975 as in 1974 (35.1 percent compared with 34.9 percent). In reviewing the allocations, I was concerned to see that unrestricted grants to higher education dropped slightly from 1974 (6.9 percent to 6.7 percent), although there was a compensating increase in departmental and research grants (5.2 percent to 5.4 percent), which probably reflects increased corporate emphasis on specific academic programs.

Business can do a good deal better, especially in the light of higher profits realized over the past two years. I would urge that business launch a two-pronged effort to raise the levels of *financial* support to higher education, especially in the unrestricted grants area, and to consider innovative ways to provide support *in-kind*. It should reach out through nontraditional channels to less business-specialized scholars and find mainstream jobs for them in business that have comparable functions or require parallel skills (e.g., why not historians as investment analysts, musicians as computer specialists, teachers as salesmen, trainers, and administrators? Business could be more creative in providing facilities for universities. Equitable, for example, has cooperated with Pace University and Marymount Manhattan College in a program in which certain classes are taught at the Equitable Home Office building in midtown Manhattan. Joint programs, business and academic people "in residence" can help. Equitable is looking into the academic in residence idea now.

In conclusion, business can help higher learning in many ways— it can be more inventive in helping people attend and in raising financial support. There really is no choice if we wish to continue to enjoy the manifold benefits of education in our society.

They Say You Can't Do It, But Sometimes That Doesn't Always Work*

ROBERT L. PAYTON

SOME APPROACHES TO RAISING FUNDS from corporations are guaranteed to work—sometimes. I've known fund raisers who never seemed to vary their routine: find the closest approximation of a contributions officer and ply him with alcohol. Match him, drink for drink.

Others never get far enough from the office even to do that and instead send letters—form letters, addressed "occupant"—to everyone in whatever directory comes to hand. Others cultivate influence—find one of your trustees who knows a director of a corporation, and let nature do its work. Still others run greater risk by trying to trade the prestige of trusteeship for a grant or two; bring a corporate executive onto your college's board of trustees, but assure him first that you don't want him to help with fund raising, that you just want his advice.

Almost everything works sometimes, and that includes all the above. But as corporate philanthropy has become larger in scope and importance, it has taken on other qualities that presidents, trustees, and development officers should bear in mind.

Comparing my days in development more than a decade ago with my recent introduction to the other side of fund raising, many things have changed for the better. Corporate philanthropy is much better organized. The Council for Financial Aid to Education and the Conference Board, on one side, and the Council for the Advancement and Support of Education and others, on the other side, have by now spread a great deal of information around about how fund raising from corporations ought to be done.

There are more corporate executives paid to know something about the varieties of programs as well as institutions that might qualify for support. There is a great deal of watching and noting what other companies are doing—just as the *Chronicle of Higher Education* reports regularly on how other colleges are doing.

More companies than ever have guidelines for their contributions programs, and although many don't publish them, you shouldn't assume that guidelines don't exist. Corporations are sensitive to stock-

* Casey Stengel

holder criticism, and general reporting standards reflect a far greater degree of openness than was true even ten years ago. The presence of outside directors often encourages that openness, but there is also a change in management attitudes.

The amount of information about corporate, foundation, and corporate foundation giving is greater than it has ever been. The enterprising fund raiser will likely have too much information to absorb rather than too little. Not too long ago most of us depended on F. Emerson Andrews as the only dependable source; now we can add a whole mailing list of periodic reports and other useful information.

Because there are professionals—in the sense of paid, full-time specialists—on both fund raising and grants, the process is becoming more rationalized at every level.

Two maxims should be kept in mind: *Intrasystem goals come first* and *People don't buy Buicks because General Motors needs the money.* The first is drawn from *Systematics* by John Gall,[1] and it reminds us that contributions officers have standards to be concerned with and channels of communication to respect. To bypass a contributions officer is to demean his role. Exercise caution, *His* intrasystem goals come before yours. The second maxim comes from Sam Goldwyn (or some other mythical figure) by way of Joe Nyquist, erstwhile commissioner of education in New York and rabid collector of folk wisdom. It is the most succinct expression yet of the principle that egotism does not pay.

Corporate giving is often rational, disinterested, even well informed. You can never be sure that that is the case, but it is a safer and wiser assumption than believing corporate giving is venal, self-serving, uninformed, and whimsical.

Having been forced to convert sow's ears into purses myself at one time or another, I know only too well the pitfalls of hyperbole. So I caution you to adopt an Ernie Lombardi attention to fundamentals. Prepare your case so that it can stand on its own merits even without oral argument.

1. Follow the guidelines if you can find out what they are.
2. Prepare a solid argument, in nontechnical language, with a carefully reviewed budget.

1. *Systematics: How Systems Work and Especially How They Fail* (New York: Quadrangle Books, 1977).

3. Enlist the help of trustees *if* they're willing to become well informed. (An uninformed trustee is even less help than a letterhead trustee.) Don't, however, bypass the contributions officer.
4. Ask.

There has been a great deal of change in corporate support of higher education during the quarter-century of the Council for Financial Aid to Education. I came to my present role having known about Frank Abrams' key role in mobilizing corporate support before I knew the Exxon (then Esso) Education Foundation existed. Alfred P. Sloan and Irving Olds were tall figures in those days.

The thrust originally provided by a relative handful of corporate executives has been sustained for twenty-five years. Leadership is now in the hands of a new generation of managers, some of whom were only beginning their careers when CFAE declared that the long-term well-being of higher education and of American corporations were related. In spite of the shocks that have been felt by both institutions in recent years, the argument still holds firm.

Corporations and Colleges: Their Mutual Expectations

STEPHEN H. FULLER

I WANT TO DISCUSS the expectations that two great social institutions may legitimately have of one another—institutions with distinctly different roles in society but with great and significant areas of mutual interest and with many common elements in their recent history. Under such circumstances, it is not unreasonable to suggest that the parties can come to an agreement about their expectations of one another and arrive at a sense of common purpose that can benefit not only both of them but the nation as a whole.

First, let me review the common experiences of industry and education since World War II—experiences that should give us a basis for building effective relationships. For a considerable period after that war, we in industry and education enjoyed sellers' markets. There were more customers than could easily be supplied, and the sounds of expansion and development that accompanied this phenomenon were reassuring.

Then, as the winds of social change began to stir up the dust of our traditional bailiwicks, we found ourselves faced with unaccustomed demands, untraditional customers, uncertain markets, and a growing body of government regulations—all of which impinged upon our internal operations.

As the tempo of these changes accelerated, much of our earlier sense of family or collegiality in organization gave way to a new factionalism, which made organizational administration unprecedentedly difficult. Even as the worst of the turmoil began to subside, we were suddenly confronted with the hard realities of galloping inflation and the energy crisis, coupled with the prospect of a declining world market for *all* our services and a stagnation in the economy generally. Now we are *both* faced with a lesser share of a smaller pie. Our only salvation in such a situation is to be sure that the quality of the pie is excellent!

Given this condition of affairs, what can education legitimately expect from industry? It can expect industry to help ensure the high quality of the pie with financial aid where it is available; with professional expertise where it is helpful; with cooperative job opportunities, internships, and other work experiences for able students where these are needed. Education can expect, also, that such support will not presume changes in the nature or the philosophy of an educational institution. Industry understands the need for bodies of self-governing scholars who make their *own* decisions in the light of their institutional purpose.

The obligations of education

I subscribe wholeheartedly to the principles set forth by Hennig and Jardim in their recent best seller, *The Managerial Woman,* that true leadership must be preceded by learning to "trust in, depend on, and delegate to" others of demonstrated competence. In recognizing these rights—indeed, these obligations of education—we are also declaring that industry understands the role of dissent in education as well as the multiplicity of functions fulfilled by educational institutions.[1]

We do not correlate education with simple vocational or skill training. Industry has use for a variety of educated persons. We recognize, also, education's right to expect industry to use your product—the graduates of your institutions—in a responsible way. It is our intent to continue what the colleges and universities have begun and to help their graduates to grow and develop to their full potential in the world of tomorrow, now being called "The Learning Society." Such an intention ensures that industry will share the areas of education's social concern.

What can industry legitimately expect from education? At General Motors, we are keenly aware of the need for each organization to reexamine and reconfirm its purpose; to establish priorities for itself; to reject trying to be all things to all people; and, instead, to seize the reality of doing certain limited things well.

In short, industry can expect education to manage with what Alfred North Whitehead called "the habitual vision of greatness," striving constantly for its own unique excellence. Excellence in our time has become in some circles a dirty word, equated with elitism. To insist on excellence is to be anti-democratic, to foster inequality, even to be un-American.

Congresswoman Barbara Jordan emphasized some very unfortunate results of such thinking in a speech at Boston University in June 1977 when she received an alumni award. She said in part:

> We have been so brainwashed by an erroneous definition of democracy that we [in Congress] have difficulty prescribing any program or formula, or giving any grant which is better or more than some other grant, because we do not want to be accused of being anti-democratic. . . .
> As members of Congress, we should not be engaged in a leveling process. We ought to enunciate and promote those policies which would lead absolutely, categorically, and without hesitation to the best this country has to offer.

Such striving for excellence will force institutions of higher learning continuously to review their institutional purpose and to recommit themselves to those goals they know to be right and essential, while

1. Margaret Hennig and Anne Jardim, *The Managerial Woman* (Garden City, N.Y.: Doubleday, 1977).

at the same time discarding the unnecessary, the irrelevant, and the unworthy. Institutions of higher education can be expected to learn to manage by *objective, not* by *crisis*—to have a strategy, a plan for maintaining and advancing their goals. In short, industry can reasonably expect them to manage so that such resources as it may be able to commit to higher education, such sacrifices as parents may be prepared to make to send students, and such support as alumni and friends may strive to provide will all be used with maximum effectiveness to attain established goals. Such effective employment of existing resources can only bring more support from more sources and greater opportunities for fulfilling a mission.

What industry can expect

Industry can also expect that educators will continue to be—as they have been so often in the past—innovators, path-finders, experimenters—and not only in the sciences and technology. Many of the thorniest problems in industry today are those upon which the social sciences, psychology, philosophy, and history can throw great light. In matters, for example, of affirmative action, industry is largely involved with changing *attitudes,* which will, in turn, change behavior in a kind of circular pattern. Industry's need to eliminate certain traditional attitudes toward women and minorities as managers is as great and as immediate as its need to provide these groups with the skills they need to perform management jobs well.

Edwin Delattre of the National Humanities Faculty writes:

> When a person studies the mechanics of internal combustion engines, the intended goal is that he should be better able to understand, design, build, or repair such engines, and sometimes that he should be better able to find employment because of his skills—and thus better his life. These are no mean goals.
>
> When a person studies the humanities, the intended result is that he should be better able to understand, design, or repair a life— for living is a vocation we have in common despite our differences. . . . A realist is not a cynic, but rather a person who respects factual knowledge and its uses and is, therefore, effective. An idealist is not a fool, but rather a person who recognizes that factual knowledge is not enough to live a life. When we achieve both, then knowledge and principle inform our ordinary commonplace behavior and thought. . . . It is in this sense that the study of the humanities is said to make life good.[2]

2. *Chronicle of Higher Education*, October 11, 1977, p. 32.

And so, in our common desire to "make" life good, we in industry have the right to ask those in education to identify the problems of our society early and to point the way to possible remedies. If education will be the laboratory, industry will be the clinic. There is a kind of confusion about the basic tenets of our American Declaration of Independence. We talk equality and liberty as if they were synonymous. It can more accurately be said that equality is people enjoying common rights, while liberty is the individual's use of these rights to achieve a particular goal. If our society is to enjoy both, education and industry must walk hand in hand.

Voluntary Support: Retrospect and Prospect

HAYDEN W. SMITH

There has probably never been a time when there was not a financial crisis of some kind in higher education.* In large part this is a result of the fact that there is almost always too little money to do all the things that educators believe should be done. As one observer put it, "Education always runs at a deficit. Often, the higher the quality of education, the greater the deficit. No school or college budget ever could be termed satisfactory. The money available is never 'enough.' If more money were available, more could be done. There is no such thing as a fixed production goal in education."[1]

This being the case, it is not surprising that there has been a steady stream of commissions, committees, task forces, and individual investigators concerned with the problems of financing higher educa-

---

* This paper is a revised and updated version of an earlier paper on the same subject. See Hayden W. Smith, "Prospects for Voluntary Support," *The Corporation and the Campus*, ed. Robert H. Connery (New York: Academy of Political Science, 1970), pp. 120–36.

1. Fred M. Hechinger, "The Foundations and Education," in Warren Weaver, *U.S. Philanthropic Foundations: Their History, Structure, Management, and Record* (New York: Harper, 1967), pp. 410–27.

tion and making recommendations for the solution of these problems.[2] Many of the proposals are designed to influence public policy. They focus on the future financial needs of both students and institutions of higher education and typically show a substantial gap between those needs and the resources that would be available without new and enlarged programs of financial assistance from government. Little if any mention is made of the possibility of increasing the flow of private gifts and grants as a means of closing the gap in whole or in part.

Yet voluntary support of higher education is as old as higher education itself in this country, and it has played a major role in the evolution of American higher education for more than three hundred years. Although its recent growth has not quite matched the explosive upsurge of institutional needs in the past quarter century, its growth in this period has been phenomenal by historical standards and nothing short of extraordinary in comparison with the growth of the gross national product and other economic indices.

With the cessation of rapid growth in higher education itself, the outlook for institutional and student needs is for a much lower rate of growth in the near future than there has been in the recent past. Presuming a continuation of national policies designed to stimulate private philanthropy, the prospects are that the voluntary support of higher education will grow much faster than college and university expenditures.

2. See, for example: Joint Economic Committee, Congress of the United States, *The Economics and Financing of Higher Education in the United States: A Compendium of Papers Submitted to the Joint Economic Committee, Congress of the United States* (Washington: Government Printing Office, 1969); R. H. Atwell and C. W. Atwell, *Adjustments of the Major National Universities to Budgetary Distress* (1970); G. Hudgins, et al., *People's College in Trouble: A Financial Profile of the Nation's State Universities and Land-Grant Colleges* (Washington: National Association of State Universities and Land-Grant Colleges, 1970); William W. Jellema, *From Red to Black?: The Financial Status of Private Colleges and Universities* (San Francisco: Jossey-Bass, 1973); National Commission on the Financing of Postsecondary Education, *Financing Postsecondary Education in the United States* (Washington, 1973); Earl F. Cheit, *The New Depression in Higher Education* (New York: McGraw-Hill, 1971); and *The New Depression in Higher Education—Two Years Later* (New York: McGraw-Hill, 1973); Howard R. Bowen and W. John Minter, *Private Higher Education* (1st and 2nd Annual Reports), (Washington: Association of American Colleges, 1975 and 1976); Andrew H. Lupton, et al., "A Special Report: The Financial State of Higher Education," *Change* (September, 1976), pp. 21–38.

The history of voluntary support

Little can be said about the annual volume of financial support received by all institutions of higher education from private sources before 1910. The U.S. Office of Education did not begin to issue periodic statistical reports until 1870, and for twenty years the tabulated data contained no financial information. Although some data regarding income and property were collected after 1890, it was not until 1910 that the statistical reports included information on the amount of private gifts and grants received by colleges and universities. A clear picture of the growth of voluntary support is, therefore, available only for the last sixty-six years.

It is certain, however, that private giving to colleges and universities was a vital element in the financial picture of higher education before 1910. Despite the lack of comprehensive statistics for all colleges and universities, the records of individual institutions provide a graphic account of the importance of voluntary support both in the founding and in the preservation and expansion of higher education in the United States over a period of 272 years. Data compiled for the period 1893–1916 show that gifts of $5,000 or more to all forms of education amounted to more than $1 billion; this figure is equal to more than 70 percent of the total income of higher education during these years, and while the exact portion of these gifts going to colleges and universities is unknown, it was undoubtedly substantial.

Beginning with 1910, some information regarding the annual level of voluntary support of higher education became available, and with the passage of time the data were more and more comprehensive. Even with allowance for changes in coverage and concept, these data reveal a significant growth in the overall total of identifiable gifts and grants, increasing from a little more than $23,000,000 in 1910 to more than $258,000,000 in 1950.[3]

The tenfold increase in philanthropic support during these four decades is impressive, but the significant aspect of this growth is that it implies a small increase in the relative importance of private giving in the context of an expanded higher education. The growth of private gifts and grants was faster than the growth of faculty and enrollment and faster than most other sources of institutional income. As a consequence, private support received per student increased from an aver-

3. U.S. Department of Health, Education, and Welfare, *Digest of Educational Statistics, 1968* (Washington: Office of Education, 1968), p. 95.

age of $65 in 1910 to $97 in 1950; the ratio of total support to total faculty also increased by about 50 percent in this period.

There were also marked shifts in the relative importance of the principal purposes for which voluntary support was given. In 1910, nearly half of the total was earmarked for endowment and other non-expendable funds; by 1950 this proportion had fallen to a fourth. Gifts and grants for current operations, by contrast, rose from less than one-sixth of the total in 1910 to nearly one-half in 1950.

Voluntary support since 1950

Information regarding the amounts, sources, and purposes of private financial support of higher education has improved markedly in the past twenty-seven years. The advances in this area are the result of an enlargement of the statistical activity of the U.S. Office of Education, the National Center for Education Statistics, and the direct surveys of voluntary support conducted by the Council for Financial Aid to Education (CFAE), under a cosponsorship arrangement with the Council of Advancement and Support of Education (CASE) and the National Association of Independent Schools (NAIS).

The growth of private philanthropy in support of higher education between 1950 and 1966 was nothing short of phenomenal. The grand total of gifts and grants in 1966 was 5.8 times the amount in 1950, implying an average annual rate of growth of 11.6 percent. By comparison, the average growth rate during the period 1910–1950 was only 6.2 percent a year.[4] As was the case between 1910 and 1950, the significance of the rapid growth of support after 1950 lies in its relation to the expansion of higher education generally.

It appears that the growth of private gifts and grants between 1950 and 1966 was identical to the growth of the overall financial requirements of the institutions of higher education. Again, the comparison is more meaningful for the components of private educational philanthropy than for the total. Giving for current purposes increased 12.1 percent a year on the average, while the current operating expenditures of colleges and universities increased at an average rate of 11 percent annually. Capital gifts for physical plant and equipment, on the other hand, grew at an average annual rate of 11.9 percent, while

4. Growth rates were determined from data found in U.S. Department of Health, Education, and Welfare, Office of Education, "Biennial Survey of Education in the United States"; "Higher Education Finances, Selected Trend and Summary Date"; and "Higher Education General Information Survey."

the capital outlays of higher education appear to have risen by more than 14 percent a year on the average.

Gifts for endowment and other nonexpendable funds continued to fall as a proportion of total voluntary support. In 1966, such gifts amounted to a little more than one-fifth of total gifts and grants. The cumulative book value of endowments for all colleges and universities was $8.8 billion at the end of 1965–66, compared with $2.6 billion in 1950. Although the yield on endowment investment improved slightly in this period, the earnings from endowment in 1966 were only $356 million, a little less than 3 percent of total current-funds revenue. This represents a further decline in the importance of this source of income in the financial picture for higher education.

Beyond 1965–66 the only available clues regarding the further development of educational philanthropy are in the data provided by the Surveys of Voluntary Support of Education, since the data compiled by the National Center for Education Statistics no longer include any gifts and grants to the various capital funds. From the data furnished by the institutions participating in these surveys, total support for all institutions of higher education was estimated to total about $1.4 billion in 1965–66, increasing to about $2.4 billion in 1975–76.[5]

These data indicate clearly that there has been a major slowing in the rate of growth of voluntary support since the mid-1960s. These estimates show a growth of 67.3 percent for the ten-year period 1965–1975, or 5.3 percent annually, on the average. The rate of growth of voluntary support since 1966 has thus fallen to less than half the level of the period from 1950 to 1966, when it averaged 11.6 percent a year. With the possible exception of 1969, for which information is incomplete, the percentage increases in every year since 1966 have been smaller than the average growth rate in prior years.

The cause of this slowing down in the rate of growth is not clear. Several factors* appear to have been at least partly responsible, and taken together they are likely to have accounted for a significant portion of the result. The campus unrest of the late 1960s and early 1970s is often cited as a strong negative influence on donors' motivation, and it does seem likely to have been a factor. Of greater importance, in all probability, is the Tax Reform Act of 1969 and other subsequent changes in the tax incentives for individual philanthropy. The most

5. Council for Financial Aid to Education, *Voluntary Support of Education* (New York: various dates).

pervasive factor is undoubtedly the major alteration in the economic climate in the United States; the period since 1965–66 contrasts sharply with the preceding sixteen-year period in rate of economic growth, in economic stability, and in the degree of utilization of economic potentials. And there are other factors that may well be involved.

Whatever the explanation, the slowing of the growth of voluntary support has serious implications. First of all, it should be noted that the growth of college and university expenditures averaged 11.4 percent annually between 1966 and 1976, which was about the same as in the sixteen years after 1950. Although much of this exceptionally high rate of increase in the most recent period is a result of the impact of accelerated inflation, it nonetheless reflects a growing need for funds that has not been matched by the growth of voluntary support. As a consequence, the relative importance of voluntary support in institutional budgets diminished steadily after 1966. A second point to be made is that there are clear signs of resistance to the continued rapid growth of the other major sources of college and university income.

It is evident, for example, that colleges and universities are encountering increasing difficulty in raising tuition and other student fees, in obtaining substantial increases in state and local government appropriations, and in persuading the federal government to expand its financial assistance to institutional budgets. Should the growth of these principal sources of institutional revenue actually fall behind the growth of financial needs, then it would become an imperative to stimulate the growth of voluntary giving or to trim the further expansion of current budgets.

The prospects for an expanded rate of growth of voluntary support vary somewhat as between the various sources of support, and it is therefore necessary to examine each of these in detail.

Sources and purposes

The outstanding feature of the growth of voluntary support is that the percentage distribution by source has been fairly stable, at least since 1955, when the Surveys of Voluntary Support began. With only a few exceptions, the relative importance of the various groups of donors has fluctuated within a narrow range, and the trends of growth for the support provided by these groups have all been roughly the same as for the total.[6]

6. Ibid.

Individual donors (both alumni and nonalumni) have consistently been the largest single source of voluntary support, accounting for between 44 percent and 49 percent of the total. On the average, total giving has been split between alumni and nonalumni individuals. Next in importance after individuals are the general-welfare foundations, whose educational grants have aggregated about one-fourth of the total support. These grants, however, have fluctuated more widely, both in dollars and in percentage, than the support received from other sources.

Corporate contributions to institutions of higher education, including gifts and grants by corporate foundations, have regularly constituted between 14 percent and 17 percent of total voluntary support. In addition to the direct support of colleges and universities, business corporations also provide significant amounts of aid to education in the form of scholarships, fellowships, and support of education-related organizations that add perhaps 40 percent to their total.[7]

Among the remaining sources of voluntary support, grants from religious denominations are most noteworthy. These include support from official church bodies, church auxiliaries, church service groups, and cash contributions from members of religious orders. Support from these sources has declined from nearly 10 percent of the total in the mid-1950s to slightly more than 5 percent in the mid-1970s.

Other sources not included in the above categories included a variety of associations, service clubs, fund-raising groups, and other organizations. These diverse sources accounted for nearly 11 percent of total voluntary support during the 1950s; their share fell to about 6 percent in the 1960s and early 1970s, and in recent years has returned to roughly 8 percent.

One of the fundamental divisions of educational philanthropy is support for current operations versus support for capital purposes, including endowment and other nonexpendable funds. The most significant observation about the trends in this division is that, while gifts for endowment and other capital funds dominated the picture in the early years, gifts for current operations have increased in relative importance and since about 1970 have exceeded giving for capital purposes. Support from alumni and nonalumni individuals, however, has traditionally favored capital gifts; that from other sources has been

7. Council for Financial Aid to Education, *Corporate Support of Higher Education 1975* (New York: 1977).

heavily oriented toward support for operating budgets. While these preferences still hold true, the shift away from capital giving toward current support has involved all groups of donors.

Distribution of support among institutions

One of the major dimensions of voluntary support is the distribution of funds among colleges and universities that differ in terms of control, level of instruction, enrollment, type of program, and other factors. The data from the Surveys of Voluntary Support of Education provides the best available picture of this distribution, even though the participation rates among different classes of institutions vary markedly and the changes in institutional classification tend to make comparisons somewhat unsatisfactory.

The most significant change, however, is clearly the long-term shift in the shares of voluntary support received by public and private institutions. The private colleges and universities have dominated the picture historically, and they continue to receive a disproportionate percentage of total voluntary giving. In the past quarter century the growth of voluntary support for private institutions has been lower than the growth of total voluntary support, and the private colleges and universities have been losing ground in relation to the public institutions. In the mid-1950s, for example, the private universities and colleges accounted for about 85 percent of total voluntary support; by the mid-1960s, this share had fallen below 80 percent and in the academic years 1975 and 1976, it was just below 75 percent. Over the same span of time, the share of total voluntary support reported by public institutions rose from roughly 15 percent to slightly more than 25 percent.

Although the data have not been tabulated by level of instruction or by enrollment, it is clear that the larger institutions account for the bulk of private giving. The major private universities, for example, regularly account for about 40 percent of the total dollar amount reported by all institutions, and the public universities' share of the total has risen to more than 22 percent. Thus the universities, which predominate in graduate instruction and research, account for nearly two-thirds of all voluntary support, even though they represent only about 6 percent of the number of institutions of higher education and enroll only one-third of all students.

At the other extreme, the two-year junior and community colleges, which represents about one-third of the number of institutions and one-third of total enrollment, receive no more than 2 percent of the voluntary support of all higher education.

The four-year colleges and specialized institutions, which comprise nearly 60 percent of the number of higher educational institutions and enroll about one-third of the students, account for slightly more than one-third of voluntary support. Although the private colleges enroll less than 30 percent as many students as the public colleges, they outnumber the public colleges better than three to one and receive more than ten times as much voluntary support.

Factors affecting the growth of voluntary support

In an analytical sense, the growth of voluntary support for all higher education reflects the growth of resources available to the various groups of donors, the changes in the proportions of those resources that each donor group collectively is willing to devote to philanthropy, and the variations in the ways in which these groups are induced to distribute their philanthropic dollars among the many causes appealing for funds. The available data suggest that the first of these factors is by far the most important in explaining the growth of educational support; the proportions of their resources that donor groups are willing to give have been generally quite stable, and the distribution of total philanthropy among major categories of recipients has changed only within narrow limits.

Ideally, potential resources for philanthropic purposes should be measured in terms of both wealth and income. In the absence of any usable data on wealth, the only suitable and meaningful measure is income. For the nation, national income is the appropriate concept.

The growth of total philanthropic giving over the past twenty-five years has obviously been much more closely related to the growth of the national income than to the increase in the proportion of income that the nation allocates to private philanthropy. Indeed, since 1970 the share of income given over to philanthropic uses has declined to about the 1960 level, so that all of the growth in philanthropic giving in the last sixteen years is explained by the growth of national income. The ratio of philanthropy to national income, however, has been significantly higher since 1960 than it was in previous years. This increase is wholly attributable to foundations and business corporations; individual philanthropy has remained at a relatively stable level.

Contributions and gifts by living individuals constitute the bulk of total private philanthropy. This source of funds accounted for 87 percent of all philanthropic giving in 1950 and between 75 percent and 80 percent since 1960. Such giving amounted to $23.6 billion in 1976, compared to $3.8 billion in 1950; the increase amounts to about 524 percent, or 7.3 percent per year. This growth is almost entirely explained by the rise of personal income, which increased by 512 percent over the period.

Philanthropic giving by bequest also exhibits a high degree of stability in terms of the resources available for distribution, that is, the total gross estates of decedents. Information on this subject is less complete than for other sources of giving, since it is limited to data from only those estates for which tax returns are required. The tax data appears to be adequate for an evaluation of trends, however. These figures show that the growth of charitable bequests is almost entirely a result of the increase in the total value of estates; the share of gross estates given over to charitable bequests has fluctuated between 4.5 percent and 7 percent for more than forty years without any noticeable trend.

The total of gross estates (and charitable bequests) has grown roughly tenfold since 1950. This extraordinary rate of increase appears to reflect a combination of four factors:

1. an increase of 37 percent in the number of deaths,
2. a significant increase in the proportion of deaths requiring the preparation of an estate tax return,
3. a sixfold increase in the number of estate tax returns filed, and
4. an increase of nearly 25 percent in the size of the average gross estate.

In view of the prospective continuation of economic growth, of further aging of the population, and of the structure of estate taxation, these same factors seem likely to continue to cause further disproportionate increases in total estates and philanthropic bequests in the future. The Tax Reform Act of 1976, however, may result in some discontinuity in the growth rates, since it includes a major change in the structure of estate taxation.

In contrast to the stability of giving by individuals as a share of the resources available to them, the ratio of charitable giving to re-

sources available has shown a marked increase in the case of foundations and corporations.

For the private philanthropic foundations (excluding corporate
foundations), the appropriate definition of resources available is not
easy to establish and the information that can be assembled is not complete. The income of foundations, however, is derived principally from
endowment investments, which means that the growth of property income in the United States will serve as an indicator of foundation income.

The growth of property income between 1950 and 1976 amounted
to more than 300 percent; on the other hand, the growth of foundation
philanthropy in this period was approximately six times this much.
Clearly the growth of income is not sufficient to explain all the growth
of foundation philanthropy.

A more likely explanation lies in the rise in the number of private
foundations. Although an exact count is unavailable, there were nearly
30,000 tax returns filed by such entities in 1973, and this number appears
to be more than three times the number that would have been filed in
1950 had the filing requirement been the same. What this growth in
the number of foundations means is simply that the foundation has
been used increasingly as a vehicle for channeling funds for philanthropy from individuals to the ultimate recipients. This is borne out
by a phenomenal growth of total foundation assets, the net effect of
which is an increase in the foundations' share of total property income.

In the case of business corporations, the picture is similar to that
for foundations. Total corporate contributions to philanthropic activities increased from $217 million in 1950 to an estimated $1.3 billion
in 1976, an increase of nearly 500 percent. Net corporate income before
taxes, on the other hand, increased from $42.6 billion in 1950 to $156.9
billion in 1976, an increase of only 268 percent. Clearly the growth of
corporate income is not adequate to explain the growth of corporate
philanthropy. Corporate contributions increased from 0.59 percent of
pretax net income in 1950 to 0.83 percent in 1976.

This increase in the share of income that corporations are willing
to put to philanthropic uses is an important development. It reflects a
significant departure of corporate policy from previous positions of long
standing. Among the factors responsible for this shift are a general
change in attitude toward social responsibility on the part of corporate
management, a clarification of both the common law and the statutory
provisions regarding the power of corporations to make donations for

philanthropic purposes, and a growing belief that the long-term self-interest of the corporation and its stockholders would be enhanced by certain kinds of philanthropic pursuits.

While both corporations and foundations, as donor groups, have in fact increased the share of their resources that they are willing to devote to philanthropy, the two groups combined represent such a small fraction of total philanthropy that these changes have not yet had an appreciable impact on the ratio of total philanthropy to national income beyond the 1950–1955 increase. The stability of individual giving continues to dominate the national picture.

Given the rise in total philanthropic giving and the changes in its distribution by source, the growth of voluntary support of higher education reflects the changes in the proportions of total giving that the various donor groups are willing to allocate to higher education as opposed to other areas of philanthropy. The historical record of educational support as a percentage of total philanthropy is not precise, but the available evidence makes it clear that this percentage has increased substantially for all groups of donors. In rough terms, the share of higher education in the philanthropic dollar rose from about 6 percent in 1950 to about 11 percent in 1964, and it has stabilized around 10 percent in the past nine or ten years.

In summary, the factors that affect the size of voluntary support have all tended to cause an increase in the flow of private gifts and grants to higher education. The growth of resources has been most important in explaining the growth of total philanthropy by individuals. Although this factor has been important also for foundations and corporations, it has been less important than the increase in the share of their resources that these groups allocate to philanthropy. And for individuals and corporations, higher education has succeeded in attracting a rising fraction of the philanthropic dollar. In no case during the period since 1950 have any of these factors operated negatively for any of the donor groups.

Future trends in voluntary support

The total expenditures of institutions of higher education in 1986 are projected at $59.6 billion expressed in 1976 prices.[8] This figure implies an increase over 1976 of 33 percent *exclusive of any inflation*.

8. Martin M. Frankel and Forrest W. Harrison, *Projections of Education Statistics to 1985–86* (Washington: Government Printing Office, 1977), pp. 69–71.

Assuming an inflationary factor of 5 percent annually, the compound effect over a ten-year period amounts to 63 percent, and this would imply 1986 expenditures of more than $97 billion. If the voluntary support of higher education accounts for the same proportion of expenditures in 1986 as in 1976, then the flow of support in 1986 would need to increase to $5.2 billion. An increase to $9.2 billion would be required if the support-to-expenditure ratio were to return to its actual level in 1966. In the context of past experience and probable developments, how likely is it that between $5.2 billion and $9.2 billion of private support will be realized?

The answer necessarily involves some speculation, but the history and other dimensions of voluntary support provide useful guidelines for narrowing the range of speculation to a degree which is acceptable for most purposes. There is, first of all, the probability that voluntary support will grow because the economy will grow and because educational support, along with other kinds of philanthropy, grows with the national income.

Although a projection of the national income is beyond the scope of this paper, one may extrapolate in order to determine the potential margins within which the likely course of developments will fall. Such an extrapolation based on the 1966–1976 experience of the U.S. economy suggests that the $5.2 billion figure would barely be attained.

The national income grew at an annual rate of 8.1 percent between 1966 and 1976; a continuation of that rate to 1986 would yield a figure of nearly $3 trillion. If the ratio of total philanthropy to national income remained at the 1976 level of 2.16 percent, then total philanthropy would amount to nearly $65 billion in 1986. And if the ratio of educational support to total philanthropy remained at the 1976 level of 8.2 percent, then the voluntary support of higher education would amount to about $5.3 billion in 1986.

It is important to note that this results from a set of assumptions that is very reasonable. The growth of national income, including inflation, need grow no faster in the next decade than in the last. And both the ratio of total philanthropy to national income and the ratio of educational support to total philanthropy need not change. Other things being equal, the voluntary support of higher education will grow to $5.3 billion in 1986 simply as a result of the income effect.

Other things, however, will almost certainly not be equal. Developments of the past in regard to philanthropy generally, and in regard to giving to colleges and universities in particular, indicate clearly that changes are likely to occur in the philanthropic share of national income and in the higher educational share of total philanthropy. Both ratios have been higher than their levels of 1976, and both ratios have tended to rise with the passage of time. The prospects are that they will increase in the future.

As to support from the business community, there should be some modest increase above current levels, if only because a relatively small fraction of the corporate entities have accounted for a disproportionate share of past business giving. As more and more firms reach a significant size, there will be a larger fraction of all companies giving to philanthropic purposes at commensurate rates. This upward movement along the corporate income scale has undoubtedly been one of the influences behind the past growth of the ratio of business contributions to business income, and there are good prospects for some continuation of this phenomenon over a future span as long as ten years.

The appeal of higher education in the context of total corporate contributions has increased very considerably since 1950. Much of this reaction has undoubtedly been pragmatic in character. Business has experienced chronic shortages in the supply of technical, scientific, and administrative talent—in fact, of qualified labor generally. The growth of business support of colleges and universities has in part been merely an effort by the individual firm to ensure that it would have competitive access to college graduates in their programs of recruitment. In part, also, such support has been a concomitant of the knowledge explosion, and for many industries the productivity of funds allocated to research has been much higher for university-sponsored programs than for in-house efforts. The trends in both of these areas have been for more rather than less business aid to education, and more to such an extent that higher education has received a growing share of the contributions dollar from the corporate community.

In addition, the institutions of higher education have succeeded in obtaining a growing share of corporate philanthropy not only as a result of growing professionalism and skill in the academic development activity, but also because of growing professionalism and orderly administration on the part of the corporate contributions function. One significant change in the organization of corporate philanthropy since World War II is the gradual shift, still in progress, from passive to active program administration. Business firms now seek out, with full-time personnel and on an ever-increasing scale, new opportunities for the effective application of their contributions dollars in all areas of philanthropy. And in a competitive sense, the institutions of higher education have a slight advantage over other recipients. They can provide the corporate contributor not with opportunities to make charitable donations to worthy causes, but with opportunities to make intangible investments of a philanthropic character, which yield demonstrable long-run rates of return to the donors comparable to those from tangible investments of a conventional, profit-oriented character. The preference for the latter type of corporate giving is obvious, and it helps to explain the uptrend in the higher-education-to-total-philanthropy ratio for the corporate community. Corporate support of health and welfare is designed to treat symptoms, while higher education treats the problems themselves and offers the hope of long-run solutions.

Foundation patterns will undoubtedly change appreciably from the recent past, although the precise character of the change may not be apparent for four or five years. The Tax Reform Act of 1969 included a large number of provisions that have affected the attractiveness of the private foundation as a philanthropic vehicle for wealthy individuals. It circumscribed the operations of existing foundations through an intricate set of rules, some of which affect the potential flow of funds for philanthropic purposes. Although the long-run effect on philanthropy is still not completely clear, it seems highly unlikely that there will be any reduction in the ratio of foundation philanthropy to foundation resources unless there should be further major changes in the law. While some such changes are certain, there is no current indication that they are likely to have a significant impact on the role of private foundations in total philanthropy.

Much the same kind of stability is probable in respect to the share of foundation grants going to higher education. The most likely prospect here is for a continuation of the past volatility. As with corporations, the appeal of higher education in the grants programs of foundations may well grow stronger in the next decade. Foundation giving is generally less conventional than corporate and individual philanthropy, however, and its seems probable that innovative and experimental projects will continue to command an important share of foundation interest, perhaps even a growing share. Certainly the competition for foundation funds among the principal classes of recipients will not diminish. And the inherent lumpiness of large grants as seed money for new ideas suggests that the educational percentage of all foundation philanthropy will continue to vary significantly.

Whatever the future patterns of voluntary support from corporations and foundations, it is almost certain that support from alumni and nonalumni individuals will grow at least as fast as in the past. There is a strong probability that the overall ratio of contributions to income for individuals will return to the higher levels of the early 1960s and then rise even farther. The modest growth in this ratio since 1950 is in part a result of an upward movement of income per capita that increases the proportion of individuals at various higher income levels. As individual incomes rise, there are two factors that tend to increase contributions faster than income. The first is simply the fact that the individual has increasingly more discretionary power over the disposition of his income as his income rises. This is particularly true for income levels above $20,000–$25,000 a year. Second, the progressive structure of personal income tax rates and the deductibility of contributions from taxable income reduces the net cost of giving at the margin, and this reduction increases sharply at higher income levels. Hence, some further rise of the ratio of individual philanthropy to personal income should be expected as a result of future growth of per capita income.

This assumes, however, that there are no major changes in the income tax incentives for charitable giving. Tax reform legislation, however, is certain in 1978 and highly probable in the years beyond. Most of the changes to date have tended to depress the incentives for philanthropy, and there may well be some continuation of this trend, not as a result of deliberate efforts to curtail the flow of charitable giving but as a byproduct of tax simplification.

Historically, much of the rise of the overall ratio of contribution to income for individuals is probably a result of the success of various philanthropic recipients in appealing to the generosity of individual givers. Some of this success is due to moral progress, to higher standards of social welfare, and to greater impulses toward humanitarian action. Some of it may also be the result of an extension of the concept of self-interest to include elements of the well-being of the less fortunate and aspects of public health and education and other matters external to the individual. But a part of this success is almost certainly a result of improvements in the techniques of fund raising and to increases in the skill with which these techniques are applied. Although new techniques of fund raising and further improvements in old ones may encounter diminishing returns, there is no reason to believe that recipient organizations and institutions will not achieve some additional success in persuading individuals to expand their levels of support.

Assuming that total individual philanthropic giving does rise in the future, what can be said about the share that would flow to higher education? Objectively, it is possible to find important influences that will operate favorably for higher education.

The principal factor is education itself. The appeal of higher education for philanthropic support is basically rational, not emotional. It involves a somewhat advanced degree of sophistication to understand fully the nature and magnitude of the benefits of voluntary support for education. Consequently, further increases in the levels of educational attainment of the older age groups in the population, which contain most of the potential individual donors, will indirectly raise the relative attractiveness of giving to higher education as compared to all other causes.

This factor will be reinforced by a growth of college alumni, both in absolute numbers and as a proportion of the working population. In the past twenty years, alumni support has amounted to about half of all voluntary support from individuals, and it has been the most stable source of educational contributions. Given the continuing high levels of college enrollment, which must result in a disproportionate increase in the number of alumni, and at least a constant proportion of alumni providing support, it follows that the number of alumni donors is certain to increase in the future. Given also the past record of growth of dollar support from alumni, the close ties between college alumni and the institutions of higher education, and the element of self-interest, it would seem likely that the share of higher education in the total philanthropy of individuals will increase during the years ahead.

On balance, therefore, the outlook is favorable for some further increase in the share of higher education in total philanthropy. It is significant that the probability of this taking place is highest for individuals, for this carries the greatest weight in the determination of the overall result. Although the extent of this prospective improvement is uncertain, one may hazard a guess that the ratio will increase to between 12 percent and 13 percent of total philanthropy. And if total giving does in fact reach a level of $65 billion or more by 1986, then the voluntary support of higher education would amount to approximately $8 billion.

If achieved, this flow of voluntary support to the institutions of higher learning will provide an essential underpinning to the financial requirements of colleges and universities. It would constitute roughly 8 percent of the income likely to be needed in 1986, a proportion higher than achieved in the late 1960s but comparable to that prevailing in other past periods. More important, it would provide the basis for a less significant increase of involuntary support, that is, governmental appropriations from tax sources. The value of such a potential development bears on the quality of future social developments for the entire country.

The Dwindling Enrollment Pool: Issues and Opportunities

MARTHA E. CHURCH

THOUGH A MODEST BABY BOOMLET is being produced right now by couples who for various reasons delayed having children until now, it is doubtful that the number of babies involved will make a significant difference in the total group of young people (17–21 years of age) who will be a part of the traditional student recruitment pool of America's higher education institutions in the 1990s. Current census data that cannot be disputed suggest that this pool will be at least 25 percent smaller by 1990 than it is today. What many college and university administrators may not realize, however, is that the military will be recruiting a sizable number of eligible male high school graduates as early as the 1980s. A recently issued report of the Education Commission of the States task force on education and the military notes that

> the voluntary armed services depend on education as a recruitment tool (in contrast to education as a veterans' bonus) . . . and that if some projections of the manpower needs and expectations of the military for volunteers are met, as many as one-third of the male high school graduates of the country may receive their introduction to postsecondary education while in the military.[1]

Thomas W. Carr, former director of Defense Education in the Office of the Assistant Secretary of Defense for Manpower Reserve Affairs observes:

> If one assumes that the United States will need to maintain an active-duty military force of approximately 2.1 million, and that women will continue to join the services at approximately the present rate (40,000

1. Edwin Edwards, *Final Report and Recommendations: Task Force on State, Institutional and Federal Responsibilities in Providing Postsecondary Educational Opportunity to Service Personnel,* Report No. 94 (Denver: Education Commission of the States, 1977), p. 1.

a year), then the military . . . must recruit about one of three male 18-year-olds annually if it is to maintain an all-volunteer force.[2]

Carr adds that

the actual percentage needed in FY 1985 is 39 percent of qualified and available 17- to 22-year-old males . . . this eliminates mentally and physically ineligible (persons), those in mental and penal institutions, etc., and full-time college students . . . and . . . if reserve requirements are also considered, the Department of Defense must attract 1 of every 1.9 in the same category during the period 1985–1990.[3]

As a member of the Secretary of the Navy's Advisory Board of Education and Training, I have been particularly impressed by the Navy's need to recruit and train young people who can understand the workings of highly sophisticated machinery and weapons systems. In most cases, because of limitations in dollars, manpower, and space aboard ships and submarines, the same young people must be able to maintain the equipment they operate. The Naval Education and Training Command has made monumental progress in identifying systematically the skills and knowledge required in a number of occupational areas and it has also personalized its instruction where appropriate and manages a number of its training programs by computer. However, it still faces the same recruiting challenges of its sister services. Equally important are its continuing losses of highly skilled manpower to better paying civilian positions. This loss of workers to civilian jobs magnifies recruitment difficulties and places all of the services in stiff competition with one another and with civilian institutions for talent of varying degrees.

When one puts census data together with military recruitment needs, the outcome is predictable. An unbelievably difficult admissions crunch will be felt very shortly by all sectors of postsecondary education. Are higher education institutions ready for the challenges? Have we a valid enough understanding of the ramifications of these issues to plan properly for the future? What other issues must be considered as well?

Recruiting sixteen-year-olds

Higher education institutions may atttempt a variety of alternatives to meet the challenge of a dwindling pool of traditional appli-

2. Thomas W. Carr, "Education in the Military: A Look into the Future," mimeographed (Washington: Department of Defense, 1977), p. 1.

3. Ibid., p. 16.

cants and competition from military recruiters. Underlying each alternative will be basic issues that have important implications for higher education. For example, a number of institutions may plan to recruit and enroll large numbers of fifteen- and sixteen-year-old high school students. Will community school boards and tax agencies be both willing and able to accommodate such a change? Will postsecondary education institutions plan adequately for the needs of these young people? Simon's Rock Early College in Great Barrington, Massachusetts, has made fifteen- and sixteen-year-olds its prime constituency. The college's leaders have undertaken to recruit limited numbers of students from this age group only after carefully planning for their special needs.

Many institutions may decide that more transfers and adult students are the answer to the admissions crunch. Are primarily residential institutions capable of making the necessary adjustments for the educational, scheduling, counseling, and financial needs of adult students? Will institutions with high percentages of tenured faculty be able to respond quickly enough to meet the education needs not only of traditional students but also of the nontraditional learners?

Any legislation enacted by Congress that extends the retirement age or eliminates it may affect admissions. Such legislation could be interpreted by young people to mean that fewer positions are available for them. Making the case for a college education, particularly a liberal arts education, may be even more difficult than it is today. Moreover, many of the smaller institutions are already deeply involved in direct-mail promotion programs; how will they ever survive the extreme recruitment pressures that all education institutions—public, independent, and profit-making—will experience when the military begins to step up its recruiting efforts?

Presently, the military services purchase some education and training services from civilian institutions. Will the Department of Defense continue this practice or will it suggest other patterns for meeting its education needs? What are the implications of the recent challenges about the quality of some of these contract programs? As competition for contracts and/or students becomes stiffer, will quality be a consideration at all?

The effect of statewide planning, which carries with it the prospect of some educational programs being neither approved for public institutions nor recommended for independent institutions, is unclear.

Will such planning be a help or a hindrance to an institution recruiting for a new program that may mean the difference in an apparent life-or-death struggle? State coordinating boards have already begun to make such decisions and recommendations in Louisiana, Maryland, and New York, for example.

As states move to meet many other pressing needs, will there be sufficient funds for helping students gain access to the public as well as to the independent institutions of their choice? If not, the admissions situation becomes all the more grim for the independent sector.

Will institutions have any resources whatsoever to address some of the new education needs that are being identified by Alvin Toffler and his colleagues in *Learning for Tomorrow: The Role of the Future in Education.*[4] Topics which might be addressed include (1) how science and technology might organize the future; (2) how the post-industrial society exercises control; (3) the limits of prediction; (4) the future of sex and marriage; and (5) theories of futuristics.

Will the movement for better information for student choice make institutions struggling to survive more or less willing to reveal negative findings about their education programs as well as other aspects of their operations? Though honesty may be the best policy, one administrator has suggested that the pressures to survive may cause it to be supplanted by the "doctrine of sufficient truth." Is half-truth what students are seeking?

Some institutional opportunities

Given the prospect of an admissions squeeze, what opportunities of averting it really are available to most postsecondary institutions? The institutions that stand a good chance of meeting the challenge of radically changing enrollment are the ones that (1) have carefully delineated mission statements; (2) engage in short-term and long-term planning; (3) budget carefully and as openly as possible; (4) conduct longitudinal studies of the student population as well as systematic follow-up studies of graduates; (5) use soundly developed marketing techniques where appropriate; (6) assess education effectiveness; and (7) report this information as fully as possible to varying publics. The institutions that do only some of these activities may fare less well

4. *Learning for Tomorrow: The Role of the Future in Education* (New York: Random House, 1974).

because they will know far less about their operations and their opportunities.

Mission statements that apply to today's institutions must be reconsidered in light of tomorrow's demands. Hood College, for example, which is a liberal arts college for women in Frederick, Maryland, has just adopted a mission statement that affirms its *primary* commitment to being a contemporary liberal arts college for women. The mission statement says that Hood will serve as a lifelong learning center where women can examine, evaluate, and plan their lives, assisted by uniquely designed programs, unified resources, and faculty members carefully selected for their teaching excellence and concern for the development of the individual. The statement makes clear that Hood's *secondary* commitment is to serve the area in which it is located. Therefore, the college's programs, facilities, and personnel and material resources are available to both female and male residents of the surrounding area. Thus, through its undergraduate, graduate, continuing education, summer, and other programs, Hood has committed itself to serve as a resource center for the Frederick community. As president of Hood, I can say we know who we are, where we are going, and why. We expect to maintain the college's current student population, which has nearly trebled (with no significant change in Scholastic Aptitude Test scores) since 1972–1973, and we believe we recognize the challenges involved in "predicted changes in enrollments." To accomplish our goals we are attempting to understand fully the constraints within which we must work. In addition, we are making cautious assumptions about issues and enrollment trends of the 1980s.

Short- and long-term planning

Hood, like many other institutions, is now fully engaged in a continuing process of short-term and long-term planning. As academic, facility, and fiscal priorities are identified, we at Hood know we must consider the limitations in serving adult students. Hood cannot be all things to all students. Its academic programs are rooted in the liberal arts, and its internships are rooted academically in the world of work. Changes in academic areas will be incremental, whereas financial aid programming as well as student recruitment and student activity programming can and must change radically over the next few years. The college has begun to serve a number of adults and will continue to do so for years to come. Classrooms are now used all day, all evening, and on a number of weekends. Resident students, however, have mixed feelings about the increased use of the campus because traditional student activities have always been scheduled in the late afternoon and evening. Since Hood's faculty members were instrumental in making possible the trebling in enrollment since 1972, most are receptive to the scheduling changes mandated by a changing clientele. But scheduling and student programming are areas in which change may be difficult on a number of residential campuses.

For recruiting and other purposes, the importance of conducting longitudinal studies of the student population as well as systematic follow-up studies of an institution's graduates cannot be over-emphasized because these studies are the principal components of any assessment program.[5] Though the process is time-consuming, an institution, no matter how large, should periodically assess its educational effectiveness. Various testing agencies are hard at work developing evaluation instruments that can be used both by the very large and by the very small institution. Research psychologists such as K. Patricia Cross and Arthur Chickering are looking carefully at the new learners, including adult students, and the impact of various educational processes on them. Gathering hard and soft data on educational effectiveness is expensive but essential to the well-being and future planning of all institutions of higher education. Administrators and faculty members can no longer assume that institutional goals are being met simply because students come to our campuses and leave later on. We must know, for internal planning and for external purposes, what differences our institutions are making in the lives, knowledge, and skills of the persons, younger and older, who spend some time at one of our institutions of higher education. How else are we to know whether or not we are succeeding in meeting our stated goals?

Another opportunity for overcoming reduced enrollment relates to noncollegiate-sponsored education. Administrators need to provide their colleagues with as much information as possible about the amount of education and training taking place elsewhere in our society—in industry and in voluntary organizations and a number of governmental agencies. The American Council on Education's Office on Educational Credit, the New York Board of Regents (the New York State Educa-

5. Arthur W. Chickering, "Research for Action," in *The New Colleges: Toward an Appraisal,* ed. Paul Dressel (Iowa: American College Testing Program, 1971), pp. 25–52.

tion Department), the California State University and Colleges, and the Department of Education of the Commonwealth of Pennsylvania are cooperating in a project on noncollegiate-sponsored instruction. With financial support from the Fund for the Improvement of Post-secondary Education and the Carnegie Corporation, this project has been designed to assist education institutions to assess what academic credit might be assigned to some of the courses available within the Bell System, the New York Police Department, the YWCA, etc. More work needs to be done in this area of translating noncollegiate courses into academic credit, but this particular project goes far to help not only individual learners but also the institutions to which they may wish to transfer courses for credit.

Outreach programming

Outreach programming offers another opportunity for recruiting students that is well-known to all community colleges and most urban institutions. Now, many residential colleges, such as Hood, can and should make significant contributions of academic programs and community service to their respective communities. For example, Hood's Department of Physical Education, Recreation and Leisure Studies developed a summer camp program for one hundred patients of the county diagnostic center for mentally and physically handicapped citizens, so they would have an opportunity to do things (such as camp out overnight, ride horses, and swim in a pool in specialy constructed aquatic center with ramps for wheelchairs) they had never done before. Persons over sixty years of age pay only $25 for taking courses at Hood on a space-available basis. The college has agreed to house the instructional materials resource center for the local school system, and it has entered into other cooperative arrangements with neighboring colleges. The college's internship program, which places sixty to a hundred students a semester in a variety of agencies and organizations throughout the Middle Atlantic states, provides opportunities for student learning and service. In return, the college gains new friends, more knowledge of neighboring organizations, and a better understanding of the needs of the geographic area in which it is located.

Whenever possible, presidents and deans should encourage their faculty and staff colleagues, as well as selected students, to seek membership on accreditation teams that visit other campuses. Faculty, officers, and students who have had such an experience acquire a broader perspective on institutional philosophies and concerns. Quite possibly such experiences can open their eyes to the need and possibilities for innovations and improvements in the educational process on their own campuses.

In light of the predicted enrollment changes, each institution should reassess its review and reward structure to emphasize fostering the individual talents of faculty members and officers and undergirding individual learning of students. Research universities obviously will differ greatly from small liberal arts colleges on this issue of performance review and reward, but it needs to be addressed on each campus in the United States, particularly in view of the coming enrollment decline.

One of the most difficult problems to solve in shoring up enrollment relates to financial aid for older students. College Scholarship Service forms are not constructed for the housewife who is interested in completing a baccalaureate degree. State student aid formulas rarely acknowledge the needs of part-time students. Funding guidelines that are appropriate for younger students become irrelevant for the older part-time student who also works. A national organization or a special task force should consider this problem very carefully so that new information on such students can be provided soon to decisionmakers at the local, state, and federal levels.

In all that we in higher education do, however, we must not water down our standards. As K. Patricia Cross notes:

> We should organize education around the premise that we must demand of each student the highest standards of performance in the utilization of his or her talents. But if we are to meet the demands of our patrons and our customers, we shall have to make room for the development of a much wider range of talents than that called for by traditional higher education.[6]

6. K. Patricia Cross, "When the Customers Want a Change," *AGB Reports,* July/August 1977, p. 28.

Changes in Enrollment:
The Consequences

HAROLD L. HODGKINSON

ONE OF THE GIVENS in higher education these days is that colleges and universities are about to face an unprecedented decline in "conventional" student registrations. This decline is not a new phenomenon. It has occurred in the country's elementary schools; elementary school administrators and teachers have quickly learned a number of new skills regarding "moth-balling" school buildings and how to deal with the problems of a drastically reduced student population load. The trend is now well into the high school years and high school personnel are beginning to discover how to deal with it. When it hits the colleges around 1980, most college administrators will not be in a position to learn from the elementary and secondary professionals because of the peculiar lack of communication across sectors of the traditional American education system.

Demographic change is one dimension of the problem of declining enrollments. The valuable American Council on Education report, "Changes in Enrollment by 1985," by Cathy Henderson, points out that enrollment changes will be handled very differently in different states, based not only on the relative size of the eighteen-year-old population within a state, but also on the net migration of college students either coming into a state or leaving the state to study.[1] It is important to realize that states do differ widely in these factors. According to the Henderson report, colleges and universities in the "sun belt" states will be the winners in picking up additional students, but they enroll such a small percentage of the total college and university population that these numbers have to be interpreted with caution.

Significant variations in population occur *within* many states; for an institution that has primarily local or regional draw within a state, the picture may be quite different. (For example, one school district in the state of Washington has a population that will decrease by 40 percent during the next three years; just a few miles away, another school district, because of a new military installation, will triple its

1. Cathy Henderson, "Changes in Enrollment by 1985" (Washington: American Council on Education, 1977).

student population in the next three years.) Some small colleges, particularly in the Appalachian region, draw their students from not more than a fifty-mile radius. These institutions clearly should not rely on the national data nor even on the state-level data for their planning. Rather, they should look specifically at the region from which they draw their students.

Changing high school curriculum

Another important trend related to who goes to college is the changing high school curriculum. During the past decade, the number of high school course titles has increased from 1000 to 2000. The new course titles look very much like the ones offered during the first two years of college—Introduction to Sociology, The Film as Art Form, etc. Partly because of the "back-to-basics" movement, this high school curriculum trend will reverse. But it will take considerable time.

One indicator that a return to basics is in the works is the recent decline in "frills" in secondary education, even foreign languages. The degree to which the back-to-basics movement captures the attention of school boards across the country will determine to a large extent the number of high school graduates who will adequately meet the requirements for conventional four-year college admissions. If courses continue to proliferate, many entering college freshmen may feel they have already covered most of the college material, possibly increasing attrition. If the minimal competency standards now being developed by virtually every state in the union for high school graduation carry teeth, some people who could afford to go to college may be prevented from doing so because they have not passed the minimal competencies to get out of high school. Whether the minimal competency standards will produce more adequately prepared college freshmen is a question at this point. A commitment seems to be increasing in high schools to reading, speaking, writing, and computing, but years must pass before these trends are visible in college freshmen. The Bowen-Minter Report on the private sector schools indicates that although the entering students do well on motivation and conscientiousness and reasonably well in the humanities and sciences, faculty report that students' skills in mathematics, reading, and particularly writing are at a low level.[2] Since no nationally recognized test of writing

2. Howard R. Bowen and John Minter, *Private Higher Education* (Washington: Association of American Colleges, 1976).

ability exists, the Bowen-Minter data need to be taken very seriously. High schools are not equipped to teach people how to write; once colleges take this mission to heart, they may have to start flunking more students. Now that faculty members realize that each student has a price tag around his or her neck, and that that price is directly related to their own salaries, it is highly unlikely in public or private institutions that college grades will drop to the point where 15–20 percent of undergraduates will fail each year. While Scholastic Achievement Test scores were plummeting college grades were climbing almost as much so that the median grade in college is now almost a *B*. If some of the test scores that predict performance are dropping precipitously, but the average performance as measured by grades is increasing just as precipitously, something is clearly wrong, with the tests, with the grades, or with both.

One of the most important demographic changes affecting enrollment is related to differential fertility. The recent population decline has been carried primarily by the white and middle-class sectors of American life, while birth rates among many ethnic minorities and lower social class groups have remained almost constant. A rising percentage of young people may be from backgrounds that would indicate their having some problems with the education system. Such a situation would seem to offer an ideal time to renew the dedication to providing adequate remediation for all entering college students who need it rather than simply deciding to flunk them out in large numbers.

Talent exists across a wide array of areas, and nothing would improve higher education as much as being more specific about the kinds of talent it rewards and how its identifies talented performances. The National Assessment of Educational Progress, which is one of the best indicators of what is happening in the education system, shows that students in secondary schools know the basic skills, but they do not know when to apply them, given a particular set of circumstances and a problem presented to them.[3] Students know *how* but not *when* to add and subtract, which may be the first outcome of the high school curriculum shift. Maybe students with slightly better skills will be entering college, but they still will be weak in this fundamental competency of being able to read a problem and figure out what is needed to solve it.

3. "Report on Student Progress" (Denver: NAEP, 1977).

Peripheral organizations

An additional set of problems relating to "human ecology" and the American family will affect college enrollment. For example, last year in the District of Columbia, more abortions occurred than live births; of the live births, more were to unmarried than married women. The ultimate consequences of these shifts in life patterns on young children are not easily calculated. But they are as important as the demography itself.

The National Center for Educational Statistics in "The Condition of Education—1977" reports that about 11 million students were in colleges and universities in 1975–76, while 17 million adults were engaged in "adult education" not in a college or university.[4] Correspondence schools, vocational schools, and other noncollegiate postsecondary activity claimed almost 2 million additional students. Thus, what we refer to as the "periphery," meaning those institutions that educate people past the compulsory age for staying in school but that are not accredited colleges or universities, is actually the mainstream in that they enroll more students than the "core" does.

Several changes are likely in the "periphery" that should be considered as people in higher education seek to attract new markets. A recent report by the Conference Board indicates that the nation's largest companies spend more than $1.6 billion annually for in-house education of their employees.[5] Others estimate the figure as high as $100 billion. This figure does not include the $220 million used for tuition refund programs and $180 million for other outside courses taken by employees. There is little doubt that this number will increase in the industrial sector. As industry discovers the cost of "fringe" packages arrived at through collective bargaining, it will turn toward producing their own resources, rather than hiring them from outside. General Motors discovered that in this last year it paid more money for employee medical insurance than it paid for steel. It is only a matter of time, therefore, until education and medical benefits will be made available to workers from company-operated facilities. The long-term consequences of this move for institutions that seek nontraditional students could be quite severe.

4. National Center for Educational Statistics, "The Condition of Education—1977" (Washington: Government Printing Office, 1977).

5. *Education in Industry* (New York: Conference Board, 1977).

The second change occurring in the "periphery" is one that could be called market segmentation. Many individuals and groups are now offering—at a very high level of quality—selected services of those normally given by colleges and universities. The College Without Walls operating in Kansas City under the aegis of Ottawa University is just one good example. This institution provides not a college degree but a series of steps that allow an adult to formulate his or her own learning contract. The college offers some instruction, as well as outreach information on other educational opportunities in the area. The advisement and assessment services for adult learners offered by Centers for Educational Brokering, many of them excellent in quality, dedication, and value received for dollar invested, are another example of market segmentation.[6] Career counseling is another need that is not being filled by current counseling programs in colleges and universities. Community colleges make more of an effort regarding counseling, at a higher level of skill, than many of their four-year college and university neighbors. As more and more attention is paid to remediation, the community college may well come forth as an intellectual leader in dealing effectively with students whose learning needs may require being met in some radical, interesting ways. Market segmentation is well under way presently in a number of areas and will undoubtedly continue. The increasing competition of the military for the high school graduate will be considerable in that the military runs some of the largest (and most effective) recruiting and instructional programs leading to careers.

An accreditation war

The third trend taking place in the "periphery" is that many of these new institutions will be seeking some form of accreditation. A small civil war over accreditation may well break out among the regional accrediting groups, the state accrediting groups, and those bodies representing professional associations. Several reports have already been issued that are critical of regional associations on the grounds that they are partial to the large institutional members and do not give adequate attention to the small and somewhat radical nontraditional programs that are now emerging. Something may have to

6. James M. Heffernan, Francis U. Macy, and Donn F. Vickers, *Educational Brokering: A New Service for Adult Learners* (Syracuse: National Center for Educational Brokering, 1976).

be done to assure fair competition in the marketplace for all institutions that are not fraudulent and that seek to educate students in a variety of ways. Our pluralistic conception of education demands that we allow programs with a wide variety of strategies to exist together.

A final trend in the "periphery" concerns the increasing ability of noncollegiate institutions to award degrees. These institutions include museums, hospitals, and private firms such as the Arthur B. Little Corporation in Massachusetts. This trend will indeed alter the enrollment patterns of higher education, significantly. Students may be able to get a degree through a museum and accomplish an excellent internship that prepares them for a career in the field as opposed to following a strictly academic course in which they spend little time experiencing firsthand the problems of museum management. The outcome may be that many of the social service and cultural professions may come to demand the legitimacy that such a degree offers, thereby shifting enrollment patterns considerably.

The higher education community can respond to the changes affecting enrollment that have occurred in the "core" and "perhiphery" institutions in many ways. Most important is that colleges and universities achieve a greater specificity of mission if they are to compete effectively in what is becoming a pluralistic consumer-oriented market. Few colleges and universities have developed missions that are so specific that the programs reflect that mission.

Also needed are studies of attrition rates to establish more clearly than ever who leaves school and why, and what could have been done either to retain the student in the program or to make sure that the student returns at some future time to complete it. Studies that show how to retain or retrieve students may have the greatest potential for maintaining enrollment.

Vastly improved counseling facilities will have to be provided if we are going to effectively meet the needs of traditional as well as nontraditional students.

Marketing studies, both to *create* demand as well as to satisfy demand, will need to be done. Although people in higher education do not like to admit it, colleges and universities package and sell their products in much the same way as other institutions in the United States. A function of packaging is to increase demand while responsibly describing the product. Educators need to learn how to increase or create demand and still accurately describe what is going on.

"Convertibility" activities need to be undertaken, whereby the value of certain kinds of adult experiences can be reassessed and translated into traditional college credits. The new Council for the Advancement of Experiential Learning organization, under the leadership of Morris Keeton, offers a fine step in this area. In addition to solving problems of relating experience to credit, the definition of credit itself should also be looked at. It is not clear that a credit means anything more than "seat time"—that an individual sat in the presence of an instructor for a given period. It tells one little about what a person knows or is capable of doing.

Content as means or end

Several kinds of convertibility activities would be useful: better assessment of student activities and knowledge at entry to the institution or a course as well as better diagnostic assessment of student progress. Existing evaluation methods in common use do not allow for these assessments, although the techniques are available if people wanted to use them. Also useful would be curriculum outcome analysis studies to see whether content is a means to an end or is indeed an end in itself. The study of generic competencies that may underline much content could be included here.

Another response to changes in "core" and "periphery" institutions would be much better faculty load analysis. Higher education is very labor intensive, and most institutions do not know how faculty members spend their precious time. A study by L. Richard Meeth indicates that college faculty members spend more time on administrative duties than they spend on either student advising or research.[7] Good ways need to be discovered to help faculty handle their time more effectively. It is also clear that the same faculty will be around for years in institutions that are 80 percent tenured; those who will become department chairmen and engage in other administrative activities will need specific management training for such work. Budgets should not be prepared by departmental leaders who do not know how to balance their own checkbooks. Better training of trustees is also mandatory if the higher education community is to make the best use of the opportunities regarding enrollment that will be available in the next few years.

7. "Meeth-Hodgkinson Faculty Activity Inventory" is available from the department of higher education, State University of New York at Buffalo.

Interinstitutional consortia

Participation in interinstitutional consortia will be a major factor in the survival of many institutions in the near future. Consortia offer both the potential of lowered costs and the actualities of faculty renewal and a broader array of academic offerings. For many institutions, consortia may make the difference between survival and extinction.

Since 1860, people have regularly predicted the demise of the liberal arts college, and yet the institution has a remarkable tenacity. My hope is that many colleges will be invigorated by the issues currently affecting them and will achieve a new and more specific level of excellence. The community colleges also should begin to take on greater leadership and work to attain a greater specificity of excellence. Working toward excellence can only enhance the public's perception of the education profession. The problems resulting from changes in enrollment may be most severe in the universities in that they will have to become used to dealing with some forces and organizations they have not normally dealt with in the past. However, the trends affecting enrollment may well result in more dynamic and mission-specific higher education institutions that are better integrated into the communities and society that need them.

Enrollment Trends and State Coordinating Boards

T. EDWARD HOLLANDER

COLLEGE PRESIDENTS throughout the country have become interested in demography, admissions strategies, and public policies concerning institutions in financial difficulty.[1] The prospect of enrollment decline is widely accepted, though educators continue to refer to the possibility with the more delicate term, "enrollment stability."

Projections regarding enrollment stability exist through the year 2000. A study of the Carnegie Council projects enrollment growth from 8.4 million students in 1980 to 8.6 million students in 1985, then

1. The author wishes to thank Claudio Prieto and Paul Wing for their contributions in the preparation of this paper.

a slight decline to 8.2 million students in 1990.[2] Renewed growth is projected to the end of the century. Based upon an expected decline in the eighteen-year-old population, Cathy Henderson of the American Council on Education projects a modest 4.4 percent decline in the freshmen enrollments of traditional college-age students in the decade 1975 to 1985.[3] Stephen Dresch offers the most pessimistic outlook, arguing that the continuing high levels of college attendance will create a condition of "economic saturation."[4] He projects sharp declines in the mid-1980s extending for an additional decade through the mid-1990s.

Enrollment stability may be too optimistic a term to describe the enrollment outlook.

As Henderson reports, the Bureau of the Census projects that the number of eighteen-year-olds will decline from 4.2 million in 1975 to 3.6 million in 1985 and a further decline to 3.2 million in 1992.[5] The decline between 1975 and 1985 is about 15 percent, but between 1975 and 1992, it is 24 percent. These declines are based upon the number of children already born. The most pessimistic estimate projected for 1995 is 3 million eighteen-year-olds, a decline of 30 percent from 1975.[6] Enrollment stability will occur only if there are compensating increases in the college-going rate of the college-age cohort or increased college attendance by adult populations.

The demand for higher education and the proportion of the age cohort continuing on to college is difficult to predict. Both New York and New Jersey have experienced declines in "college-going" rates since 1971.[7] A Carnegie Commission study identified a strong decline

2. Carnegie Council, *More Than Survival* (San Francisco: Jossey-Bass, 1975), p. 45.

3. Cathy Henderson, *Changes in Enrollment by 1985* (Washington: American Council on Education, 1977), p. 19.

4. Stephen P. Dresch, "Educational Saturation: A Demographic Education Model," *AAUP Bulletin* (Autumn, 1975), pp. 239–47.

5. Henderson, *Changes in Enrollment by 1985*, p. 12.

6. This projection is based on continuation of the most recent fertility rate of 1.7 live births per couple. However, the expectation is that the fertility rate could rise to 2.1. If it does by 1977, then the number of eighteen-year-olds for 1995 is expected to reach 3.5 million, a number close to the 1985 level. See Leon F. Bouvier, *U.S. Population in 2,000—Zero Growth or Not*, vol. 30, no. 5 (Washington: Population Reference Bureau), pp. 18–20.

7. The college-going rate in New York declined from 65.6 percent in 1971 to 63.2 percent in 1975; (see *The Regents Statewide Plan for the Development of Postsecondary Education* (Albany: New York State Education Department, 1976), p. 15). In New Jersey, the proportion of high school graduates who are college bound dropped from 58 percent in 1971 to an estimated 54 percent in 1974; see *New Jersey Department of Higher Education Data Briefs*, No. 11 (August, 1975), p. 1.

in the proportion of white eighteen–nineteen-year-old males going on to college, from 47.3 percent in 1969 to 39.6 percent in 1972.[8] Richard Freeman reports a drop among male eighteen–nineteen-year-old civilians from 44 percent in 1969 to 33 percent in 1974.[9] Freeman explains this drop on the basis of a decline in the rate of return for investment in higher education, from 11–12 percent in 1969 to 7–8 percent in 1974.[10] High unemployment rates, increasing underemployment of college graduates, and employment of college graduates in areas unrelated to their major fields of study could continue to discourage college attendance. The number of college graduates seeking employment is expected to increase for the next five years; unless employment opportunities rise, or the real cost of higher education declines, there is little reason to expect a significant reversal of the downward drift in the college-going rate in the next five years.

Enrollment competition

In contrast, the number of older students enrolled in colleges and postsecondary institutions has risen significantly between 1970 and 1975.[11] Yet, the American Council on Education study points out that 94 percent of all first-time full-time enrollments were of people under twenty years of age.[12] While higher education institutions may seek to encourage the enrollment of older students, they face competition from school districts, public agencies, professional associations, and industry, as well as other colleges that now serve adult populations. The impact of population changes and consequent enrollment declines will vary significantly from region to region. The Henderson study points out that

> two-thirds of all freshmen are enrolled in states . . . which are not projected to experience overall reductions in the number of 18-year-olds by 1985.[13]

8. Carnegie Commission on Higher Education, *Priorities for Action: Final Report of the Carnegie Commission on Higher Education* (New York: McGraw-Hill, 1973), table A-2.

9. Richard B. Freeman, *The Over-Educated American* (New York: Academic Press, 1976), p. 34.

10. Richard Freeman and T. Herbert Holloman, "The Declining Value of College Going," *Change* (September, 1975), p. 25.

11. In 1970, 410,000 persons, aged 30–34, enrolled in college. By 1975, the number had risen to 853,000. See U.S. Bureau of the Census, *School Enrollment —Social and Economic Characteristics of Students: October 1975*, Series P-20, no. 303 (Washington: U.S. Government Printing Office, December, 1976), p. 4.

12. Henderson, *Changes in Enrollment by 1985*, p. 7.

13. Ibid., pp. 5–6.

Nine states with expected declines account for 28 percent of total enrollment. The independent college sector is especially vulnerable. Over 40 percent of enrollment in independent colleges will occur in states expected to lose enrollment, compared with 28 percent of the enrollment in public institutions.

These data suggest that the pessimists tend to live in states that (1) now enjoy high college-going rates, (2) presently enroll a large number of nontraditional students, (3) already provide open access and enroll previously underserved ethnic groups, (4) are located in an area of the country facing larger than average enrollment declines, (5) have a significant number of undergraduate liberal arts colleges, and (6) have a relatively large number of independent institutions.

New York is one such state and projected enrollments are for substantial declines beginning in 1981 and continuing into the mid-1990s. New estimates for New York State project a decline of 55,000 students between 1976 and 1985 (slightly over 10 percent) and a decline of 125,000 full-time students (about 25 percent) between 1976 and 1995.[14]

Whatever the overall trends, enrollment declines are likely to be significant for wide segments of the academic community.

Enrollment decline and institutional behavior

What is the likely impact of overall enrollment declines upon individual institutions?

Early in 1974, the New York State Education Department, as part of its statewide planning effort, developed an enrollment projection model that predicted full-time undergraduate enrollments for each college and university in the state through 1990 based upon their then existing missions and the state's financing policies.[15] Each institution's enrollments were projected by estimating its enrollment share of the expected number of high school graduates from each region of the state and from out of state. The enrollment share was estimated on the basis of "drawing power" between 1969 and 1973.

A total of 187 institutions were then grouped into five categories. The second largest category comprised Group V, the 44 institutions

14. These estimates were prepared in March 1977 for presentation to the New York State Board of Regents. Preliminary data were obtained from the Office of Postsecondary Research, Information Systems and Institutional Aid.

15. T. Edward Hollander, "Planning for Changing Demographic Trends in Public and Private Institutions," in *Assuring Academic Progress Without Growth,* ed. Alan Carter (San Francisco: Jossey-Bass, 1975), pp. 1–12.

in this group were expected to continue to maintain stable enrollments or slight growth. Institutions were classified into Group V if they accepted a small proportion of their applicants and drew 25 percent or more of their full-time undergraduates from outside of the state and at least one-half of their freshmen from outside of the region in which the institution was located. The assumption was that Group V institutions could and would maintain their enrollments by adjusting admissions requirements to maintain stable enrollments. These institutions were expected to experience a decline of 10 percent or less.

The other 143 institutions were assumed to share the remaining pool of applicants. Projections for enrollment decline at these institutions ranged from 10 percent to 40 percent or greater. Institutions with expected enrollment declines of 40 percent or more include small public and independent institutions that together enrolled only 10 percent of the state's undergraduate population. The twenty independent institutions so classified were small liberal arts colleges that had experienced severe declines since 1969. They were not expected to survive. Institutions enrolling one out of two full-time undergraduates in the state fell into the 20–30 and 30–40 percent range for enrollment decline. Half of the state's independent institutions fell within these two categories, as did most of the public two-year colleges. Independent colleges were most likely to suffer severe enrollment losses. Almost three out of four independent institutions were expected to experience enrollment declines of 20 percent or more compared with one out of two public institutions.

These projections were transmitted to all the institutions in the state, along with a detailed description of the methodology so that they could replicate the study. Those institutions that challenged the findings did so on the basis that they planned to change their recruitment and education strategies to avoid the forecasted decline.

The dissemination of this study influenced institutional plans and behavior. Several institutions shifted the emphasis of their education programs from serving college-age undergraduates to serving nontraditional age populations. Examples of such institutions are Mercy College, the College of New Rochelle, New York Institute of Technology, and Adelphi University. Several institutions developed extension and outreach centers and began offering adult and continuing education programs. Recruitment and admissions functions received greater support and emphasis within the institutions. Small liberal arts colleges began professional and career programs, and other institutions concentrated resources in expanding their programs. The competition for students among these small colleges intensified and promotional advertising became common.

The state's overall enrollment pattern has followed the initial projections fairly closely. For individual institutions, however, these projections are not likely to be realized. A number of institutions have responded to possible enrollment decline by expanding the constituencies they serve. Several institutions already have closed and their enrollments have been redistributed within the system. Several consolidations have also taken place. The publication of these data also has resulted in changes in overall financing and planning policies that will alter the outcome from the projected model.

The role of the state board

The point is that the state coordinating board can play a catalytic role simply by providing institutions with adequate information about possible trends and directions. Many, though not all, institutions can modify strategies and programs, if they are provided with adequate and credible data and have confidence in the information available. Fear for institutional survival is one of the most powerful change-agents around.

Some institutions, with sufficient lead time, can explore alternative arrangements for adjusting to enrollment decline if that is their likely future. If these institutions close, and many may, plans can be developed for their orderly dissolution and the relocation of students to other institutions.

The New York State Education Department has undertaken a project to identify more precisely institutions in difficulty or heading for difficulty so that it can intervene early enough to maintain an institution's viability or protect the students should the institution fail.

An initial effort to identify vulnerable institutions was based on the Carnegie Commission's indicators of strength.[16] The education department, based on its experience, has identified several additional measures of strength. An institution least vulnerable to enrollment decline attracts students of all ages, rather than just eighteen- to twenty-one-year-olds; provides for significant part-time enrollment; is co-educational; and qualifies for state support. It is located in an urban rather than a rural area; depends to a lesser rather than a greater degree upon tuition income; and operates at or near its planned capacity.

These characteristics have been used to identify institutions within

16. Carnegie Council, *More Than Survival*, p. 81.

the total number that need to be monitored less intensively. These criteria, by and large, have been useful as an initial screen of institutional strength. The institutions found to be most vulnerable to enrollment decline are small, rural independent liberal arts colleges, especially women's institutions, charging high tuition and operating significantly below capacity.

Developing lead indicators

A second phase of the department's efforts is the attempt to develop *lead indicators* that could be used to identify individual institutions headed for difficulty. Financed in part by a grant from the Ford Foundation, the study uses extensive profile data accumulated for each institution on applicants, acceptances, enrollments, fiscal measures, debt service, tuition levels, and space utilization. The study will attempt to identify factors that precede actual enrollment declines and/or predict operating deficits. Department staff members now review institutions' profiles periodically to identify those that need special monitoring and management assistance.

The impact of overall enrollment changes on individual institutions is difficult to predict. Enrollment declines do not fall proportionately on all institutions within a system. Further, there is no reason to believe that the academically strong institutions will survive while the academically weak ones will absorb the full brunt of an enrollment decline. In fact, the academically strong institutions may be competing with similar institutions for a given applicant pool on a regional or national basis. Declines in that applicant pool do not necessarily mean that an institution can or will shift its education and admissions efforts to serve a different applicant pool.

Experience on the impact of enrollment declines between 1971 and 1975 in New York State suggests that overall enrollment declines tend to affect a limited number of institutions, while others maintain stable enrollments or even grow. To measure and be able to predict how enrollment declines are distributed, the department staff is now examining measures of "selectivity" and "yield."

Defining "selectivity" as the ratio of acceptance to applications and "yield" as the ratio of first-time full-time enrollments to acceptances, important information can be developed and analyzed.

- Institutional selectivity and drawing power of all institutions among and within sectors can be measured by the relationship between these variables for individual institutions.

• Institutional vulnerability to enrollment declines can be measured, assuming the least vulnerable institutions are highly selective and attract a high proportion of students they accept. Institutions with low "selectivity" and low "yield" would be expected to absorb the major share of a statewide enrollment decline.

• Institutional admissions patterns can be followed over a longer period of time to identify institutional response as enrollments change, providing a basis for projecting enrollments.

In a preliminary exercise to test this approach, Paul Wing devised a matrix measuring "selectivity" and "yield."[17] Institutions were then classified along both axes as high, medium, and low for each variable, with one-third of the institutions identified in each group.

A total of 202 New York institutions—public and independent—were then distributed within the matrix. The result shows that the interplay of applications and acceptances defines 13 percent of the state's higher education institutions as being selective and competitive (high yield). Roughly 8 percent appear to be nonselective and not too competitive.

The distribution combines widely diverse undergraduate institutions, ranging from degree-granting proprietary institutions to major multiuniversities, under varying forms of governance. A differentiated scattergram based upon governance disclosed that

• The State University of New York is a diversified system with above average selectivity.

• The City University of New York is a nonselective system, below average in competitiveness.

• The proprietary institutions are nonselective, but they attract a high proportion of applicants who are accepted.

• As a sector, the independent institutions overlap the other groupings.

Institutions headed for trouble

The analysis of shifts of "selectivity" and "yield" for individual institutions or groups of institutions over a longer period of time would be more meaningful. It could serve to identify institutions headed for trouble. Wing developed a two-year series to show the technique in-

17. Paul Wing, New York State Education Department, in an unpublished study, August, 1977.

volved in such an analysis. A longer period of mapping is needed if this technique is to have predictive power. The diagrammatic portrayal of shifts between 1975 and 1976 in "selectivity" and "yield" shows

- Lower "selectivity" by the independent seminaries, and SUNY's four-year and two-year colleges. "Yield" remains unchanged.
- Lower "yields" for the SUNY Health Science's Centers and the SUNY specialized colleges.
- Increased "selectivity" and "yield" by the independent Health Sciences Centers and engineering and technical schools.
- Increased "yield" for the independent multiversities and universities with a slight increase in selectivity.
- A decline in "yield" for the CUNY senior colleges and a slight increase in "yield" for the CUNY two-year colleges.

The efforts to project enrollments and develop lead indicators to identify institutions in difficulty or headed for difficulty are important services a state coordinating board can offer to help institutions understand the implications of overall enrollment declines for their own planning.

Coordinating boards are likely to be called upon to develop measures to maintain cooperation among institutions with respect to recruitment and admissions. Uncontrolled and uncoordinated, the increased competition for students poses serious threats to the credibility of higher education and the consequent ability to maintain public confidence and public support.

A growing number of colleges and universities have adopted a new "hucksterism" in an attempt to maintain or expand their enrollments. Misleading catalogs, promotional advertising, and promises of placement have been used by some hard-pressed colleges to lure students. A number of cases have been identified of institutions awarding excessive credits for course work, recognizing life experience for credit when it is not justified, and reducing program requirements to attract students. A number of programs marching under the nontraditional banner on close examination seem to be nothing more than "credentialing" arrangements designed to meet enrollment goals and budgeted tuition revenues. A great many institutions have developed extension programs at sites far removed from their home campuses that are managed by local administrators not employed by the colleges. A cynical observer might comment that "franchising" has finally come to higher education.

Competition and conflict

Increased competition for students poses another threat. It can increase conflict between secondary and postsecondary schools as each system seeks to offset enrollment declines by extending the age group of the constituency it serves. Conflict has occurred in many states over the distribution of vocational education funds and early admissions practices and in the vying for funds to support adult education.

Finally, the competition within the higher education community has strained relations within the public sector as each institution seeks to maintain its enrollment through expanded recruitment in areas served by other public institutions.

Universities have lowered admissions criteria, seeking to attract students normally in the applicant pool for four-year colleges. Four-year colleges, in turn, have recruited students now enrolled in two-year colleges or who would normally be part of the applicant pool for two-year colleges.

Public and independent institutions in a number of states are engaged in bitter public conflict for state funds.

Another emerging danger is unplanned expansion of program offerings by some institutions beyond their program competence and resources in an attempt to capture a larger pool of applicants.

The simultaneous move of all institutions into the same program areas or to serve the same nontraditional constituencies could weaken academic effectiveness by stretching each institution's resources over more diverse areas. Unless enrollments do expand, an institution's academic and fiscal strengths are likely to be weakened. During the last five years, many colleges expanded program offerings to maintain enrollments without eliminating programs of declining demand.

In such cases, institutional resources are spread thin, institutions can no longer maintain their special strengths, and programs proliferate to the mutual disadvantage of all students.

These problems resulting from enrollment stability are likely to grow as the competition for students increases. Inevitably, such problems discredit the higher education community and increase adversely our ability to maintain public confidence and support.

It may be the institutions once fearful of coordinating boards may find in them an alternative that is less objectionable than the chaos and more pernicious government intervention that is likely to result from open conflict within the higher education community. Whatever the agent, mechanisms are needed to

- maintain minimum standards for program offerings, monitor promotional advertising, and assure adequate information is provided for informed student choice
- define boundaries and operating practices with respect to the roles of secondary schools, vocational schools, and colleges and universities in serving adult and other nontraditional students, as well as college-age students
- define more precisely the respective roles of public and independent institutions within the statewide system and provide for resolution of conflict among institutions
- establish standards and approval arrangements both for branch campuses and extension centers
- help establish consensus within the higher education community on budgetary and financing proposals or develop a common budgetary and legislative program for submission to state governors and legislatures

Easing the transition

State policies can ease the transition from enrollment growth to enrollment stability or decline.

A number of steps can be taken to increase the demand for postsecondary education by increasing access. The broadest approach is the establishment of a state need-based student-aid program, especially for segments of the population that are underrepresented in higher education because of economic barriers. Special educational opportunity programs can be more specifically directed at underrepresented populations. Evaluation of noncollegiate programs for possible college credit and expanded use of credit-by-examination can encourage increased numbers of adults to return to college. Programs developed with or for industry, professional associations, labor unions, and public agencies could encourage constituent adult groups to return to college. Student aid for part-time students could be expanded. Better information for students and simplified student-aid procedures are long overdue in all states.

States that now lose large numbers of students to institutions in other states can reduce the out-migration of students by developing more generous student-aid arrangements for in-state study and by strengthening the quality of their educational offerings. Both New York's present and New Jersey's proposed student-aid programs effectively reduce the cost of in-state study for state residents by requiring attendance in the state for maximum student-aid support.

State policy can be a major factor in determining whether public institutions or publicly funded independent institutions can use a period of stability to strengthen existing programs. Most funding formulas for public institutions and state subsidy arrangements for independent institutions are based on enrollment. Institutions are under pressure to grow in order to qualify for increased public funds.

In states that anticipate overall enrollment declines, state agencies, in collaboration with institutions, should seek to change financing arrangements that are governed by enrollment. Alternatives that should be explored include reducing budgeted enrollments and transferring funds to support existing or promising program areas; developing formulas for budget reductions based on variable costs; and developing cost-driven or program-driven models of financing postsecondary institutions.

Statewide planning for periods of expansion of higher education served higher education needs well; it is essential during periods of stability and decline. Well-coordinated planning involving institutions can establish a rational planning framework. If the process is well conceived, it can define institutional missions more precisely and assure higher education needs are met with minimum interinstitutional and intersector conflict. Strengthened coordinating arrangements can complement planning efforts.

Institutional academic and fiscal planning will be difficult unless there is a well-defined and understood system for public financing of higher education. While it is unlikely that states would abandon the annual budgetary process or forward-fund higher education institutions, states can adopt systemwide policies for financing. Principles can be developed that guide institutional subsidy levels, tuition charges, and student aid, thereby providing institutions with a basis for long-term fiscal planning. The regents in New York have developed a set of coordinated principles that guides their annual fiscal proposals.[18] Though State legislatures may not adopt definitive formulas, state coordinating boards can use them in the annual budget review.

18. *The Regents Statewide Plan*, pp. 110–24.

The influence of state policy

New York is an interesting example of the changes in public policy that could result from widespread acceptance that substantial enrollment declines are likely to occur and that state policy can influence the viability of the statewide education system.

One early response of the regents and the legislature to declining enrollment was the overhaul of the state's tuition assistance program. The new program, initiated in 1974, expanded access for low-income students to all institutions, public and independent. The generous aid program now funded at over $200 million annually provides higher award levels for students attending independent institutions. Public sector support for the program reduces considerably the tension that had been growing between it and the private sector as enrollments shifted from the independent to the public sector. The new aid program contributed, in part, to the stabilization of enrollments in the independent sector in 1974 and 1975, arresting a five-year enrollment decline. In the fall of 1976, the independent sector's share of total undergraduate enrollments rose for the first time in recent history.

A second outcome of the wide acceptance of the possibility of enrollment declines was the establishment by the regents of a special commission on the financial problems of institutions in financial difficulty. Nathan Pusey, former president of Harvard University, chaired the commission. The commission recommended

> a State policy that permits institutions, public or private, to compete under state financing policies based on fair rules of the game as they seek to attract students and serve public needs. . . . It would mean, for example, that no special state aid be granted to any institution from any source, or any authority, unless all institutions are given opportunity to present their problems and apply for such aid.[19]

Limiting political intervention

While calling for even-handed state financial policies that would permit all institutions to compete effectively for students within a coordinated statewide system, the commission also sought to keep the state from providing special aid to failing institutions. To limit political intervention to the greatest extent possible, the commission recommended that the commissioner of education establish formal procedures for in-

19. *Report of the Regents Advisory Commission on the Financial Problems of Postsecondary Institutions,* Nathan Pusey, Chairman, September 1975.

vestigating the affairs of an individual institution that has severe financial problems. The commission further recommended convening an outside group of experts, if necessary, to investigate and make recommendations on institutions in difficulty. The use of the outside panel was to limit political intervention. Among the other recommendations, the commission called for procedures for the orderly closure of ineffective and unneeded institutions. The regents accepted the principal recommendations of the commission.

It is fair to say that the regents, the higher education community, and most public officials agree that the statewide system should be permitted to contract as enrollments decline. They reject the alternative that the state should intervene with special financial aid in an attempt to maintain the existing overbuilt system. This policy has been tested in a number of cases with mixed results. Several independent colleges have been permitted to close. However, the governor and key legislators did succeed in appropriating special state aid in support of one politically influential institution.

The policy has been more difficult to implement in the public sector. In attempting to resolve CUNY's fiscal crisis, the board of higher education proposed the merger of three existing institutions and the reclassification of two four-year colleges to two-year status. The legislature overruled the board's recommendations. After the smoke cleared, one merger was accomplished and one four-year college was reclassified to two-year status.

The regents and the higher education community continue to believe that selective closures based mostly on student choice is an educationally sound strategy for accommodating expected declines.

A third outcome of the widespread acceptance of enrollment declines was the voluntary reductions by SUNY of its enrollment goals and construction programs. SUNY has adopted enrollment ceilings for most of its four-year colleges that are at or near present enrollment levels. Similarly, but also as a result of fiscal exigency, CUNY has sharply reduced its enrollment goals. Both systems will maintain open access for high school graduates through the community colleges.

A fourth response to enrollment decline was the adoption by the regents of new and tough standards for program approval to assure that existing programs meet high expectations for quality and to control shoddy program offerings developed to expand enrollments. These standards also will limit unnecessary program proliferation.

Achieving a consensus

A fifth outcome of concern for possible enrollment decline is the recent effort within the higher education community to achieve consensus on some basic principles for public financing of higher education. The effort, undertaken cooperatively through the Association of Colleges and Universities of New York and supported by the New York State Education Department and the regents, seeks to minimize potential conflict across sectors and assure a well-defined public policy that will facilitate planning by individual institutions. Agreement has been reached on the need to define financing programs to maintain the present enrollment balance between the public and independent sectors. The college community will attempt to agree on a fiscal plan for presentation to the governor and the legislature that will maintain the relative shares of financial support of public and independent institutions. This cooperation deserves special emphasis. If the leaders of all sectors of the academic community are able to define, propose, and jointly support financing and coordinating arrangements, higher education institutions will be able to gain maximum political support. Such an agreement is the most effective response to potential crisis as a divided system invites decreases in public support. The challenge to achieve unity is well understood, but a consensus across sectors has yet to be reached.

While stable enrollments may characterize future enrollment patterns for many institutions in most states, individual institutions and some states are likely to experience sharp enrollment declines of traditional college-age students. Until there is clearer evidence that the college-going rate will increase significantly, all states and institutions would do well to develop contingency plans based upon assumptions of reduced enrollments beyond 1981.

Opportunities for extending access to nontraditional populations by further lowering economic and education barriers to postsecondary education exist for many individual institutions and in some states. Even so, there is reason to doubt that extending access will alter significantly the outlook for most institutions, especially in states facing enrollment declines.

Coordinating boards can play a constructive role in collecting, analyzing, and monitoring demographic and enrollment data for the higher education community. The boards can serve important functions in monitoring institutional practices, establishing processes for orderly contraction, facilitating the development of a well-defined and coherent public policy for financing higher education, and maintaining public confidence in support of the statewide systems.

In states facing enrollment declines, the role and authority of co-ordinating boards are likely to increase, very likely with the support of the higher education community. This enhanced role will be welcome if coordinating boards are supportive of the statewide system.

Reaffirming the Value of a College Education

PETER D. BELL

DURING THE FIRST SIX DECADES of the century, the value of a college education was an article of faith, a tenet in the American credo. That many now perceive its value as uncertain raises questions not only about the experience of American college students but also about the condition of U.S. higher education and of the wider society.

Most Americans continue to believe that a college education is worth the cost. But in recent years several factors have conspired to raise doubts on the part of students, parents, legislators, and journalists. Ironically, the preeminent factor may be that the American educational dream has finally been realized: For the first time in our history, a majority of the young people in this country are going to college. But the result has hardly been the millenium. Never before has the student clientele been so diversified; the system of higher education, so overloaded; and the results of the educational process, so uneven.

Second, the post-World War II period has witnessed increasing specialization and fragmentation of knowledge. Whereas colleges once confidently designed curricula for a general education, they are more likely now to require the student to take a few distributional credits and then to settle into a single discipline. To speak of an "educated person" is old fashioned. It is far more common to talk of a "well-trained person," a concept which is given meaning in the test of the marketplace.

Third, long after most major colleges ceased being sectarian, they maintained an almost religious aura, presenting themselves as institutions set aside from the worldly bustle for the pursuit of truth, beauty, and the good life. Over recent decades, however, they have become increasingly secularized. As more explicitly political, social, and economic purposes have been thrust upon them, they have been increasingly subjected to political, sociological, and economic analyses like any other important social institution.

Economic appraisals

In the 1960s, radical students launched an attack on colleges and universities as bastions of American capitalism and imperialism. According to their Marxist view, higher education institutions existed for little more than the perpetuation of the ruling class and its liberal ideology. In the 1970s, the challenge to higher education is less political than economic. To some degree, this challenge has arisen out of a combination of inflation, recession, and demographic trends which affect all institutions but which take a particularly heavy toll on educational institutions. But it has also arisen from an overly facile application of economic theory and techniques for measuring the worth of a college education.

When they first appeared in the 1960s, the new theorists of human capital were bearers of glad tidings to university and college educators in that they provided a "hard-headed, pragmatic" rationale for increasing public expenditures for higher education.[1] More recently, however, they have been shown to practice the same dismal science as their more traditional colleagues. Having accorded credence and prestige to such economists when they brought good news, educators and politicians feel they are in no position to reject the bad news. In fact, what is required now, as earlier, is neither outright acceptance nor rejection, but rather a critical reception, with proper attention to the limitations of the underlying analysis and to the full context of the findings.

Probably the most widely cited study of the declining economic value of a college education in the 1970s is Richard B. Freeman's *Overeducated American*.[2] Its most important findings, popularized in newspaper headlines about the "Surplus of Grads," are that

> The college job market underwent an unprecedented downturn at the outset of the 1970's, with young graduates just beginning their careers most severely affected. Real and relative earnings of graduates dropped, employment prospects and occupational attainment deteriorated, and large numbers were forced into occupations normally viewed

1. For example, G. Becker's analysis of data from four census years indicated a private rate of return of 13 percent per annum and a social rate of return of 25 percent. See *Human Capital* (New York: National Bureau of Economic Research, 1964), pp. 112 and 120.

2. New York: Academic Press, 1976.

as being below the college level. For the first time in recent history the economic value of an investment in college education fell.[3]

At first glance, Freeman's study seems a sweeping indictment of American college education, and it does bring to the surface issues which ought to concern students, parents, educators, and policy-makers. Nevertheless, when put in context, the findings are less damaging than is suggested by the book's startling title.

In the first place, Freeman himself qualifies his findings, pointing out that the depressed market for graduates reduced the proportion, but not the absolute number, of young white males enrolling in college; the enrollment of blacks and women did not decline but leveled off. Second, the downturn of the early 1970s was attributable to a combination of the slower growth in industries which employ college graduates and the continued expansion of the supply of graduates. Third, as a result of affirmative action and other efforts to combat discrimination, the rate of return for blacks investing in a college education rose to exceed that of whites. Fourth, the job market for female graduates held steady, except in the case of teachers, who suffered from the delayed effect of the decline in the birthrate.

In a recent article, Leonard A. Lecht has further softened the impact of Freeman's major findings by questioning the emphasis on the earnings of recent graduates in economic studies of the value of a college education.[4] Lecht observes that, as educational level rises, the prospect of becoming unemployed diminishes. Moreover, the earnings of college graduates show a greater progression during their work life than do those of nongraduates, so that the earnings differential favoring the graduates widens with age. Lecht also speculates that college graduates may be exposed to fewer occupational accidents and illnesses and may receive more generous fringe benefits. Freeman himself acknowledges that, even with their drop in income and occupational attainment, college-trained workers have higher earnings and better prospects than their high school peers. At 7.5 percent return, a college education yields less than the 11–13 percent of the 1960s, but for most graduates it remains a sound investment.

Other appraisals

I do not question the legitimacy of the economist's concern with the measurable economic return from a college education. Attitudinal

3. Ibid., p. 184.
4. "Grading the College Diploma," *Across the College Board*, April 1977.

surveys over the last two decades show that the primary motivation for going to college is the expectation of increased earning power. This motivation may be particularly pronounced among students whose parents did not go to college, mostly minorities and members of low-income and lower-middle-income groups. Moreover, legislators and politicians generally have been solicitous in wanting to show that appropriations for education are social investments which yield tangible results for students and their families. Finally, practically oriented experience and training have a long and proud tradition in American colleges and are very properly a part of higher education.

If Freeman and his fellow human-capital theorists can be criticized, it is not for directing attention to discounted lifetime incomes and rates of return on educational investments, but for regarding them "as the critical measures of the value of schooling."[5] Economists seem sometimes to forget in practice what they know in theory: that discounted lifetime income measures only the private pecuniary return from schooling and fails to measure either the private nonpecuniary return or much of the social return. In a "non-economist's view" of the value of a college education, Harold Howe II asserts that, "when vocational objectives become so narrowly focused that the only valid measure of an educational institution's contribution to the lives of its students is found in their future incomes, then it has lost much of its claim to being educational."[6] There are, and should be, real limitations on economic techniques for assessing the value of a college education.

The economist's habit of referring to the private nonpecuniary returns of education as the "psychic income" of individuals connotes speciousness or unreality. Because economists consider psychic income to be subjective and nonquantifiable, they omit it from their calculations.[7] Nevertheless, most of us sense that such nonpecuniary returns can actually be of immeasurable value.

Aside from offering experience and training in applied areas, a college education should help to free people from the parochialism and

5. Richard B. Freeman, *The Declining Economic Value of Higher Education and the American Social System* (New York: Aspen Institute Program on Education for a Changing Society, 1976), p. 4.

6. "The Value of College: A Non-Economist's View," a Ford Foundation reprint, adapted from an address before the Atlanta Historical Society (New York, November 10, 1975), p. 14.

7. For a discussion of private and social returns, see Fritz Machlup, *Education and Economic Growth* (Lincoln: University of Nebraska Press, 1970), pp. 30–34.

boredom of their immediate situations. It should inculcate self-discipline, which is the beginning of maturity; ability to communicate articulately and logically in writing and speaking, which is critical both to rational argumentation and to easy self-expression; love of learning, which is the impetus for continuing education; and skepticism before easy answers ("the ability to detect when a man is talking rot").[8] As Frank Rhodes observes, it should also impart "an understanding of one's relationship to his total surroundings, a familiarity with other cultures, [and] an understanding of thoughts and values through the ages."[9]

In *A College Degree and What Else?*, Stephen B. Withey catalogs many of the ways in which people are changed by their college experiences. Despite the variety of colleges and the diversity of students,

> there is a general impact of college education across most institutions and most students. Students who start from a low socioeconomic base appear to change in the same areas, and in the same direction, as their more privileged peers.
> The college experience appears more likely than not to make students more open-minded and liberal, less concerned with material possessions, more concerned with aesthetic and cultured values, more relativistic and less moralistic, but more integrated, rational, and consistent. . . . [College graduates] are more introspective and concerned about personal and interpersonal aspects of life but relish more of the pleasures of interpersonal living. They have a greater sense of well-being. They tend to feel more socially efficacious and personally competent.[10]

The social returns on a college education are more than the aggregation of private pecuniary and psychic incomes. They include the benefits to other people and to society at large. They encompass the extent to which graduates have gained in their capacity to organize and participate meaningfully in social institutions, ranging from friendships, marriage, and the family to collegial relations, civic groups, and political parties. By most reckonings, graduates are able to adjust more successfully to such institutions than are their less educated peers.

8. A British professor, quoted from *The London Times* in Machlup, *Education and Economic Growth*, p. 14.

9. Quoted by Gene I. Maeroff in "The Liberal Arts Degree and Its Real Value," *New York Times*, June 12, 1977.

10. Stephen B. Withey, *A Degree and What Else? Correlates and Consequences of a College Education*, a Report prepared for The Carnegie Commission on Higher Education (New York: McGraw-Hill, 1971), pp. 129, 131.

The human-capital theorists generally focus on employment from the viewpoint of private return, but employment can also be examined as a social role, a role which is given more scope by a college education. Another social role which is expanded and made more meaningful by advanced education is that of citizen. Innumerable political science studies have shown that college graduates are more active and effective participants in the political process. By and large, they are more tolerant of deviant behavior and minority opinion, and less prone to favor violent solutions to problems. They are better informed about political issues; they take part in campaigns and vote more frequently; and they are more often elected to positions of leadership. Because education has widened the horizons of their lives, they can better understand the social and historical significance of public events, and thus they conduct themselves more responsibly as citizens, sensitive to the implications of their acts.

Maintaining a balance

I have emphasized the limitations of economic appraisals of the value of a college education and indicated the need for a more far-reaching assessment. The question "Is a college education worth it?" is, of course, rhetorical in the abstract. To be meaningful, it must be made more concrete: What kind of a college education? For what kind of a student? The most bewildering, and most promising, aspect of American higher education is its diversity. There is some kind of college education which is worthwhile for almost everyone with the intelligence, motivation, and discipline to gain admission. The real question is not whether high school graduates should go on to college, but what the overall balance and direction of higher education in America should be.

Excessive preoccupation with the employment and earnings of graduates can have a pernicious effect on the quality and values of higher education. Unfettered pursuit of truth and beauty is not automatically advanced by the search for high-paying jobs in a competitive, highly industrialized economy. At the same time, intellectual and academic excellence must not become a surrogate for social elitism. American higher education must respond in varying and inventive ways to the economic and social aspirations of its students.

Two distinct but intertwined sets of values are likely to continue their competition for dominance within higher education and the wider society. The first set emphasizes the positivistic, technocratic, and egalitarian; the other, the humanistic, libertarian, and pluralistic. As is true of the society at large, the vitality and prosperity of the overall system of higher education will depend on its capacity to encompass both sets of values and to hold them in tension and in balance with one another.

Particularly in the current economic circumstances, American higher education stands in danger of having too many of its colleges move further in the direction of trade schools. Other things being equal, government finds it more genial to support colleges as means of adding value to manpower than to support them as sources of critical ideas. Given the decline in the economic return from a college education, the federal government is feeling increased pressure to maintain the current proportion of enrollment among young people and to subsidize the educational outlay of students and their families. That pressure is likely to be strongest in behalf of the most vocationally oriented students, and increased support for them could in turn increase governmental interest in applied training.

Though they cannot ignore the economic concerns of students and their families, colleges and universities have a responsibility to resist the uncritical application of technocratic values to the polity and culture, and to affirm the significance of academic institutions as transmitters of culture, creators of knowledge, preservers of freedom, and critics of society. My confidence in their ability to do so rests in a faith that Americans can organize to demand the best of themselves and of their educational institutions; and I believe that process must start with the colleges and universities themselves. They must reaffirm the practicality of the ideal of equality *and* excellence.

What Are the Returns on a College Education?

HENRY M. LEVIN

THE QUESTION that constitutes the subject of this panel reminds me of a story I heard in Latin America: A third-grade teacher was drilling her students in addition. Little Jaimito was straining his arm upward, hoping that she would call on him. Finally she looked at him and asked,

"Jaimito, how much is eleven and eleven?" Jaimito answered, "That depends." The teacher scowled: "It does not depend; now how much is eleven and eleven?" Jaimito answered again, "It depends." The teacher groaned and asked sarcastically, "On what does it depend?" To which Jaimito replied, "Am I the buyer or the seller?"

Surely, the answer to the question "Is a college education worth it?" depends upon who is asking the question. Not only will buyers and sellers give different answers, but so will different individuals and different constituencies. In this paper, I will suggest that, on the basis of pecuniary criteria, an investment in a college education does pay off for the average individual; this view contrasts considerably with recent arguments that the private pecuniary returns from higher education have fallen to such marginal levels that this investment does not compete favorably with other alternatives. I will question, however, whether these high private returns are matched by high social returns. Finally, I will speculate about the dynamics of what is taking place and will consider the dilemma for public policy.

The individual perspective

Since the early 1960s, economists have developed increasingly sophisticated methods for evaluating investments in education.[1] In general, the human-capital approach contrasts the additional monetary earnings associated with an additional unit of schooling (for example, a college degree versus a high school diploma) with the additional costs incurred for that schooling.[2] The returns to the investment are the earnings the individual receives beyond those of an otherwise similar person who has not taken the additional schooling. The costs include foregone income (i.e., earnings that are lost during the additional schooling period by not being employed) as well as any direct costs such as those incurred for tuition, books, and so on.

By relating the increase in lifetime earnings that is associated with more schooling to the costs of more schooling, one can estimate the pecuniary rate of return on that investment in a fashion similar to such calculations for other investments.[3] In general, if the rate of return (which is expressed as an annual percentage) exceeds or equals that of

1. Gary Becker, *Human Capital* (New York: Columbia University Press, 1964).

2. Ibid., and G. Psacharopoulos, *Returns to Education* (San Francisco: Jossey-Bass, 1973).

3. *Returns to Education*, chap. 2.

alternative investment possibilities, the investment is considered worthwhile. If it is less than that of the alternatives, it is considered not to be worthwhile, unless there is some redeeming virtue not captured by the calculation. For example, some people may find that such benefits as enjoyment of the college experience and the greater prestige associated with having a college degree make the investment worthwhile even when its rate of return is lower than that of other investment opportunities.

Until recently, the internal rates of return to the individual for a college education were estimated to be in the 11–15 percent range. Since these figures are considerably above the 8–10 percent returns which represent the maximum on such typical personal investments as government and corporate bonds, an investment in a college education was judged to be a very good one. Recently, however, Richard Freeman has recalculated the rate of return on a college education and has concluded that it declined from about 11–12.5 percent prior to 1968 to as low as 7.5 percent at present.[4] His analysis has raised serious questions about whether a college education is a worthwhile investment for the individual.

Essentially, Freeman's evidence rests upon an apparent decline in the ratio of earnings between college and high school graduates; according to Freeman, the college graduate's average salary was 53 percent higher than the high school graduate's salary in 1968 but only 35 percent higher in 1973. While some of this decline can be attributed to the demographic bulge of college graduates—a 50 percent increase between 1968 and 1973—and to the recession, Freeman estimates that, even in the long run, the rate of return to a college education will be depressed relative to the earlier period. From this analysis, he concludes that the proportion of high school graduates enrolling in college will decline because many of them will not view college as a worthwhile investment.

I believe that Freeman overstates the decline in the rate of return to a college education in that his calculations reflect the deterioration in the market for college graduates but do not take into account what may be an even greater deterioration in opportunities for high school graduates.[5] Though Freeman used data on the starting salaries of recent college graduates, he failed to consider data on the earnings of recent

4. *The Overeducated American* (New York: Academic Press, 1976).

5. See my book review in *Harvard Educational Review*, May 1977, pp. 226–31.

high school graduates. Rather, he used the average earnings of all full-time workers as a statistical proxy for the starting salaries of the latter group. But the earnings of experienced full-time workers are much more likely to increase from year to year than are those of new labor-force entrants with high school diplomas because the former are more likely to be protected by their seniority, by collective bargaining and professional agreements, and by the sizable investments their employers have made in their on-the-job training. Thus, the use of this statistical proxy is likely to overstate the upward trend in the earnings of recent high school graduates.

A further bias that would tend to overstate the prospects of the high school graduate relative to those of the college graduate is Freeman's failure to take account of the large and apparently rising gap in unemployment between the two groups. While unemployment rates for college graduates, age twenty-four or less, rose from about 2 percent in 1967 to about 6 percent in 1975 and 1976, the rates for high school graduates rose from about 6 percent to the 14–16 percent range over the same period.[6]

Had Freeman obtained data on the earnings of recent high school graduates to compare with those of recent college graduates and had he adjusted for changes in unemployment between the two groups, I doubt whether he would have found evidence that private rates of return to a college education are falling. The sharp decline in opportunities for the contemporary college graduate is equaled or exceeded by the somber reality facing the high school graduate, a fact not reflected in Freeman's analysis. Thus, relative to their older counterparts, recent graduates at both levels have suffered with respect to job opportunities and earnings.

Evaluating the recent trends in the income and earnings of younger and older graduates at both educational levels, John Grasso found that the incomes of both college and high school graduates between the ages of 35 and 44 increased by an annual rate of 7 percent between 1967 and 1974, whereas college graduates under the age of twenty-four showed annual gains of only 5.7 percent and high school graduates an even lower 5.4 percent.[7] Using data from the National Longitudinal Survey that per-

6. Mary A. Golladay, *The Condition of Education*, 1977 Edition, National Center for Education Statistics, U.S. Department of Health, Education, and Welfare (Washington: Government Printing Office, 1977), p. 221.

7. "On the Declining Labor Market Value of Schooling," paper prepared for the 1977 Annual Meeting of the American Educational Research Association, New York City, April 1977, Figure 8. Paper available from the author, College of Human Resources and Education, West Virginia University.

mitted control for such factors as ability, experience, postschool training, and area of residence, Grasso also found that college graduates entering the labor market in 1970 and 1971 had actually increased slightly their relative earnings advantage over high school graduates entering the labor market in those years relative to a similar comparison for labor market entrants in 1967 and 1968.[8] Although (when adjusted for rising prices) the value of the earnings for both groups of graduates suffered an absolute decline between 1967–68 and 1970–71, the decline was slighty greater for high school graduates. Even these results may understate the increasing disadvantage faced by the high school graduates, because the comparisons are not adjusted for the apparently rising probability of unemployment faced by the high school graduate in comparison with his college counterpart.

In summary, high school graduates seem to be experiencing an even greater deterioration of economic opportunities than are college graduates, though both groups are faring badly compared with their older counterparts and with past trends. One should recall that the calculation of internal rates of return is essentially a comparison of additional benefits (in terms of higher earnings associated with more schooling) with additional costs (a significant portion of which is represented by the lost earnings attributable to continuing in school rather than entering the marketplace). As earnings for high school graduates decline relative to those for college graduates, the benefits of a college degree climb, and the costs fall.

Paradoxically, then, the rates of return to an investment in college education may be holding their own or even rising, not because the opportunities for college graduates are particularly great but because the prospects for high school graduates have worsened considerably. Thus, the available data suggest that a college education is probably still a worthwhile investment for the individual, at least from a pecuniary vantage point.

The social perspective

But even if a college education is worth it to the individual, it does not necessarily follow that it is worth it to society. To the degree that the society has costs or returns that differ from those of the individual, the social rate of return may diverge from the private one. On the cost side, the individual pays only a portion of the direct costs of his education.

8. Ibid., tables 2 and 3.

Higher education is heavily subsidized by the government, through its sponsorship of colleges and universities at the state and local levels as well as its provision of grants and subsidized loans, and such subsidization constitutes a burden on society.

On the return side of the equation, a gain in earnings for an educated individual is not a gain for society if that person merely displaces a less educated person from a job that the latter is equally competent to perform. Only when the market can provide full employment for all college graduates will each new college graduate reflect an increase in social productivity comparable to the improvement of his own position. In fact, since at least the late 1960s there have been more college graduates than jobs to employ their skills. As a result, college graduates have tended to displace high school graduates in the job hierarchy. So rapidly has this displacement occurred that between 1970 and 1975 the proportion of college graduates employed in professional and technical occupations declined from 67 percent to 60 percent.[9] Moreover, the Bureau of Labor Statistics estimates that in 1985 there will be one million more college graduates than jobs requiring a baccalaureate.[10]

According to Lester Thurow, the present situation may be characterized as one of job competition where workers are assigned a position in a queue chiefly upon the basis of their education.[11] Employers see education as a measure of trainability, for most actual job skills are acquired through experience and on-the-job training. To minimize training costs, employers select the "best" workers for the best jobs, where the worker's income will be determined primarily by the quality of tools and equipment that is available to him. Workers are then selected for jobs according to their position in the job queue, with the best jobs going to those at the head of the line and the poorer jobs going to those farther back. Those near or at the end of the line get no job at all.

In such a situation, a gain for a more-educated worker is counterbalanced by a loss for a less-educated worker, and little or no net bene-

9. U.S. Department of Labor, *Educational Attainment of Workers, March 1975*, Special Labor Force Report 186 (Washington: Government Printing Office, 1976), p. 48.

10. *Occupational Projections and Training Data*, Bulletin 1918 (Washington: Government Printing Office, 1976), p. 20. This estimate is probably conservative since it is based upon economic growth rates that may be overly optimistic and since it does not take into account the downgrading of requisite job skills for particular occupations that has been taking place. On the latter point, see Harry Braverman, *Labor and Monopoly Capital* (New York: Monthly Review Press, 1974).

11. *Generating Inequality* (New York: Basic Books, 1975).

fit accrues to society. This view is supported by evidence that, although education has become more equally distributed in recent years, earned income has not. Rather, changes in education among individuals tend to redistribute existing jobs and income among those individuals without providing a higher level of income or a more equal distribution of that income for the society as a whole.[12]

In summary, the society pays more than the individual does for a college education but does not get the same level of returns because more-educated people simply displace less-educated (but capable) people in the competition for available jobs. Thus, the social rates of return to investment in college education are likely to be considerably smaller than the private rates of return, and they may even be negative. If so, a social investment in higher education costs society more than it returns to society, at least in economic terms.

A public policy dilemma

If these data are correct, one must conclude that college education is a worthwhile investment for the individual, but not for society. In fact, the social investment may lead to increased conflict in the workplace as more and more college-educated workers find that their job expectations are not being met. As long as this nation was experiencing rapid economic growth and progressively greater demands for skilled labor, the labor market could absorb the waning flood of college graduates. Given the bleak prognosis for economic growth and the continuing high personal incentives to obtain a college degree, however, the disparity between appropriate jobs and the number of college-educated persons seeking those jobs will widen, with important consequences.[13]

Under such conditions, young college graduates will find increasingly that their job expectations are not satisfied, and thus they will not be integrated into work organizations as readily as were their predecessors. Not only does higher education tend to inculcate skills, values, and attitudes that correspond to the most prestigious jobs in the work hierarchy, but also it creates the expectation of having the high status, income, independence, and mobility that such jobs afford. But young

12. Ibid.

13. For a more detailed discussion of this assertion see Henry M. Levin, "Educational Opportunity and Social Inequality in Western Europe," *Social Problems*, December 1976, pp. 148–72. An expanded historical and conceptual analysis for the United States is forthcoming in H. Levin and M. Carnoy, et al., *The Dialectic of Education and Work*.

college graduates will find themselves competing with less-educated workers for jobs of lower prestige and income that allow only limited mobility and that are characterized by routine.

As a consequence of this divergence between the schools and the workplace, youth will grow increasingly disaffected with both work and society. High expectations will be thwarted by distasteful realities, and the resultant frustration and dissatisfaction will be manifested in disruptions of production and in lower productivity. For example, the quality of workmanship may deteriorate to the extent that quality control becomes a serious problem. Absenteeism, employee turnover, and alcohol and drug abuse on the job are likely to increase, as are work stoppages created by wildcat strikes and employee sabotage. So significant have these problems become in the U.S. that the federal government has issued its own report on the subject.[14] In short, the increasing disjuncture between the values and expectations of the educated worker and the realities of the workplace will create what Herb Gintis has called a new working class of revolutionary youth, an educated proletariat.[15]

From a public-policy perspective, there is no clear-cut way to alleviate the problem. Some economists have suggested eliminating government subsidies to college education so that the costs to the individual will rise and the rate of return will decline.[16] Such a step would reduce the demand for a college degree and bring the labor market back into balance. But this solution does not recognize that education represents the dominant path for social mobility in our society, particularly as other routes for attaining higher occupational status and income have been closed off. If access to this path is blocked; the frustration would simply be directed toward other institutions and would move into the streets, as was evident in Western Europe in the events of 1963. Moreover, this solution is particularly troublesome at a time when the higher education system has just opened up to the less advantaged.

The second alternative is reflected in the movement toward "career education," which attempts to integrate more closely the worlds of

14. U.S. Department of Health, Education, and Welfare, *Work in America* (Cambridge, Mass.: MIT Press, 1973). Also see James O'Toole, "The Reserve Army of Unemployed," *Change*, May and June 1975, pp. 26–33, 63.

15. "The New Working Class and Revolutionary Youth," in *Schooling in a Corporate Society*, Second Ed., ed. M. Carnoy (New York: David McKay and Co., 1975), pp. 293–309.

16. See, for example, Douglas Windham, "Social Benefits and the Subsidization of Higher Education: A Critique," *Higher Education*, pp. 237–252.

education and work by offering career guidance, increasing the career content of curricula, interspersing periods of work and schooling as part of the regular educational cycle, and providing a more "realistic" understanding of the nature of work and available opportunities.[17] One obvious aspect of this approach is that it attempts to reduce "unrealistically high" expectations for prestigious careers and to guide students into preparing for more attainable lower-prestige ones. Unfortunately, there is almost no evidence that such an approach will make students more "realistic" and offset the historic quest for social mobility through the educational system.[18]

A third alternative is to alter traditional educational patterns through "lifelong learning" or "recurrent" education.[19] This effort is aimed at reducing the demand for college by replacing the traditional educational cycle with one where people can take instruction at those times in their lives when they perceive the need. Of course, the relative lack of productive work for young people who leave the educational system will tend to work against their taking the recurrent education approach seriously. Whatever else its merits, recurrent education is not likely to alleviate the problem of over-education in the job market. In summary, present public-policy alternatives are unlikely to resolve the conflict, and major institutional changes in the workplace seem inevitable.

Because the possibilities of good jobs and job promotions will be limited, it will be necessary to improve the characteristics of existing jobs in order to avoid costly disruptions, quality control problems, and productivity lags. This solution has been recognized recently in both government reports and academic analysis of the existing situation.[20] Increasingly, we might expect to see various forms of worker democracy and expanding worker participation where teams of workers are organ-

17. See, for example, Sidney Marland, *Career Education: A Proposal for Reform* (New York: McGraw-Hill, 1974); and Kenneth Hoyt *et al., Career Education: What It Is and How to Do It.* (Salt Lake City: Olympus, 1972).

18. For a more general analysis, see Norton Grubb and Marvin Lazerson, "Rally Round the Workplace: Continuities and Fallacies in Career Education," *Harvard Educational Review,* November 1975, pp. 451–474.

19. Selma Mushkin, ed., *Recurrent Education,* National Institute of Education, U. S. Department of Health, Education, and Welfare (Washington: Government Printing Office, 1974).

20. See *Social Problems,* pp. 148–72; and Levin, *The Dialectic of Education and Work.*

ized to formulate, implement, evaluate, supervise, and fulfill training needs for particular work functions.[21] That is, much of the hierarchy and extreme division of labor will be reduced in favor of participative and self-governing work reforms. Moreover, these changes in work organization are likely to have a profound effect on both the nature of the work relation and its educational and training aspects. That is, in response to the changes in work organization, there are likely to be alterations of the educational system as well.[22] Thus, we should expect to see accomodations in both the workplace and in the educational sector in response to the present and future oversupplies of educated workers.

All in All—Is It Worth It?

STUART A. TAYLOR

Textron, the company I represent, is a large, multiproduct, multinational corporation which employs about 60,000 people. Almost without exception, its executives, managers, professional staff, and sales personnel have college educations; the same statement could probably be made about every major corporation in America. Providing for the world's use complex products and services that are safe and efficient requires people with the best education that this country can provide. Now and in the future, then, business will need college graduates.

But everyone who reads the newspapers has known for several years that something is amiss: The world of work and the world of academe seem to be out of alignment. According to reports, the ranks of the unemployed and the underemployed are swelling with college graduates. It is not surprising that prospective students, parents, and legislators are questioning the wisdom of committing financial resources

21. A good description of various forms of industrial democracy can be found in David Jenkins, *Job Power* (Baltimore: Penguin Books, 1974). A more analytical approach is Paul Bernstein, *Workplace Democratization: Its Internal Dynamics* (Kent, Ohio: Kent State University Press, 1976).

22. For details, see Levin and Carnoy, *The Dialectic of Education and Work*; Levin, *Workplace Democracy and Educational Planning* (Paris: International Institute for Educational Planning, 1978), forthcoming; and "A Taxonomy of Educational Reforms for Changes in the Nature of Work," in Carnoy and Levin, *The Limits of Educational Reform* (New York: David McKay, 1976), chapter 4.

to a type of education that produces graduates apparently unprepared for the world of work.

American business is not eager to point the finger at academe because it has some serious problems of its own. In this paper, I will discuss some of the difficulties that afflict business and higher education, and I will suggest some areas where business and academe might collaborate on producing solutions that may benefit everyone.

Antibusiness attitudes

Private industry has long suffered from a negative image in this country. As far back as the 1890s, corporations were blamed for the severe agricultural depression. Following World War I, a number of large corporations were labeled "Merchants of Death" and accused of getting America into the war so that they could sell munitions and other military material. Much of the economic malaise of the 1930s was attributed to "big business," a catch-all phrase that too often connotes evil throughout the private sector. Though most Americans today believe in the free enterprise system, businessmen have not enjoyed the public esteem granted to other professionals.

Unfortunately, these attitudes are widespread among young people. Many of them believe that jobs in business are not worthy goals. They view progress and new technology only in terms of their social costs, without regard for their contributions to the good life. It is ironic that a large proportion of bright and talented youth have in recent years rejected careers in business, since their entry into such careers might help improve the situation. For the problem, though partly one of communication, also demands reform from within. In simple terms, too many of the people now employed in commerce have a college degree but failed to get a college education.

The fact remains that private enterprise as we know it cannot survive in a climate of skepticism and mistrust. The restoration of public confidence is the most urgent challenge confronting business today, and that challenge cannot be met without the help of educated people.

The limitations of liberal education

Nearly four in five young people in the United States now graduate from high school; of these, well over half go on to postsecondary education of some kind. Yet fewer than half of those who matriculate receive the baccalaureate within four years after college entry. Though many of these merely delay completing their college work for a year or two, others must be regarded as permanent drop-outs. The costs of providing space and instruction for the millions of young people who never complete college are staggering, and the waste of public dollars shameful.

Why are attrition rates so high? A large proportion of young people who enter college have no sound reason for being there and would not have attended if they had been given valid information. They have no clear idea of how a college education might contribute to their vocational goals. After twelve years of elementary and secondary education, they are fed up with schooling and anxious to move out into the world. Nonetheless, they enter college because they have been urged to do so by teachers, counselors, and parents and because they can always find some postsecondary institution that will accept them.[1] When they finally come to realize their mistake, they drop out; but some damage has already been done, in terms of wasted time and effort and frustrated hopes.

Many of those who persist in college may be no better off. A liberal education is a four-year learning experience which emphasizes (1) the ideal and theoretical rather than the practical; (2) the development of personal taste in such areas as music, art, and literature; and (3) the development of a capacity for self-expression. It assumes that the student will acquire useful skills and practical knowledge in graduate or professional school or through on-the-job training. Though no one can quarrel with the goals of a liberal education, it should be acknowledged that, at least in the short run, they are not appropriate for all young people.

While not pretending to have all the answers, corporate personnel officers are concerned about the lack of meaningful career planning during the college years. They are concerned about the unemployment and underemployment of college graduates, a problem that has grown to alarming proportions. The Bureau of Labor Statistics projects a surplus of more than one million college graduates by 1985.[2] Even now, thousands of graduates must scale down their aspirations and take jobs

1. Walter Guzzardi, Jr., "The Uncertain Passage from College to Job: Education for the World of Work: III Series," *Fortune*, January 1976, pp. 128–30.
2. *Occupational Projections and Training Data*, Bulletin 1918 (Washington: Bureau of Labor Statistics, Department of Labor, 1976), pp. 20–22.

which traditionally have not required a college degree, thus displacing less-educated people further down the employment ladder.

Employers are conditioned to look at the bottom line, to ask "What skills, concepts, and ways of thinking does this college graduate have that makes him or her more desirable as an employee than the non-graduate who is available at a lower salary?" Too often, the answer to this question does not favor the college graduate, who may have a better vocabulary than the nongraduate but does not necessarily have the capacity for superior work behavior. College graduates without specialized employable skills can by and large be classified as unskilled laborers. Finding jobs for history or English majors, for example, has become as difficult as finding jobs for clerk-typists who can type only 20 words a minute.

Of all the changes that came out of the campus turbulence during the 1960s, the one that may have the most lasting impact on higher education is the demand for accountability. Audited accounts, salary schedules, course evaluations, and grades are easily accessible and quantifiable, but they are only part of the answer. The business community and the general public are much more interested in what a college education really accomplishes, what relevance it has to living and working. The definition of educational effectiveness is particularly appropriate where interpersonal work behavior and skills are involved. No matter what changes may have taken place in someone's way of thinking, if those who work with that person perceive no significant improvement in work behavior, the educational process has failed.

The answer lies not in curriculum or in teaching methodology. Too many teachers are deeply involved in abstract and theoretical pursuits and too far removed from the real world. Some of their disdain for the practical rubs off on their students, who then prefer a career that does not involve the aggressiveness, decisiveness, risk, and drive required to succeed in the business world. This does not mean that curriculum and course design are unimportant, simply that they are not by themselves sufficient components of effective education, if by "effective" is meant that some lasting and desired change is detectable in the overt behavior of the student after the education has taken place.

Many students have come to recognize the shortcomings of the present higher educational system. The large majority of America's college graduates do not go on to graduate school, and the desire for a secure future drives many into premature professionalism, unemployment, or underemployment which may be destructive of the goals of a liberal education. Perhaps more significant than these problems is the demoralization that occurs among students at those institutions which have given them responsibility for shaping their own education. A loss of faith in the value of what they have been striving to create for themselves can be devastating.

I think it is clear that what students are asking for is a problem-oriented education. They want to be able to answer questions about themselves, about their role in life, about what they can do to make the world a better place for human beings. The world seems beset by problems that our great faith in knowledge leads us to believe can be solved. We need a cure for cancer, a solution to the too-rapid exploitation of the world's natural resources, individual and collective attention to the problem of environmental pollution.[3]

College students around the country are changing their emphasis from the abstract and theoretical disciplines that were popular in the 1960s toward studies that will prepare them for careers. According to the campus correspondents of the *New York Times*, a spirit of vocationalism is flourishing, and liberal arts colleges are becoming preprofessional or pretechnical schools for students who say that job preparation is their primary reason for going to college.[4] The following is evidence of this trend:

- At Northwestern, half of the undergraduates say they are pre-med.
- Engineering is making a comeback at many schools.
- Regents at the University of Minnesota have urged that such courses as engineering, agriculture, biological sciences, and veterinary medicine be emphasized.
- As the costs of education continue to mount, and as college enrollments level off, state legislatures are urging that what money there is be devoted to studies that produce people able to do the jobs that need to be done.

3. Stuart A. Taylor, "Professional Development and People Utilization in the Future Job World," address at the Professional Development Conference, June 5–8, 1977.

4. Seymour Lusterman, *Education in Industry: A Research Report*, No. 719 (New York: The Conference Board, 1977).

- College deans claim that students appear to be more mature and realize that once they graduate they will have to make a living.

The need for a new education/work policy

Addressing the question of "education for what?" Willard Wirtz said: "Manpower need theorists trace the problem of underemployment of college graduates to some form of malfunction in the educational system; young people are being educated for jobs that don't exist."[5] There are many areas where academe can and should make improvements. I do not mean to imply that colleges and universities should discontinue liberal arts curricula. Every educator worthy of the name believes deeply in the value of a liberal education, not only as a preparation for life's pursuits and purposes but as an end in itself. Yet few would maintain that this case for college can stand alone. The heavy monetary investment involved in a higher education must always be paid by someone. American businessmen would probably agree that young people should acquire some marketable skills in college as part of that investment payoff.

Even if preparation could be perfectly matched with identifiable employment opportunities, however, a serious gap would remain. According to Wirtz: "The sterner truth has emerged: that there is not today, and will not be as long as we stay on our present course, enough employment using trained and educated young people."[6] College graduates entering the overcrowded job market must compete not only with one another but with adult women and senior citizens wanting to live more productive lives.

The unemployment and underemployment of college graduates are only part of a much broader problem that might be solved if the various troubled groups could join forces in an attempt to accomplish together what they cannot do alone. Some of these groups are

- college graduates who are currently frustrated because they have no way to use the talents that they worked so hard to develop
- men and women in their fifties and sixties who will be asked to retire earlier than they had planned

5. Willard Wirtz, "Education for What?" address at the 32nd National Conference on Higher Education, Chicago, Illinois, March 22, 1977.
6. Ibid.

- adult women who want to combine motherhood with careers but who cannot do so because of the lack of part-time job opportunities
- those well-educated people who find themselves stuck in jobs that require only a small part of what they have to offer and who want to make mid-career changes
- those people who were promised equal employment opportunities by law a decade ago and whose progress has now come to a full stop
- and, last on my list but not least, those dedicated employers searching for ways to bridge the gap that separates the world of work from academe.

The supply-and-demand model that is basic to Keynes and Samuelson seems to be the wrong medicine for our economic problems. Keynesian economics has worked well to reflate a receded or depressed economy but not to reduce inflation. Wage and price controls are not very effective either. The political system will not tolerate high unemployment for a long enough time to control inflation, nor will it accept prolonged periods of very high inflation.[7] The only way this country has survived high unemployment rates is by turning older employees out to pasture earlier and earlier and keeping young people in school longer and longer. But unemployed and underemployed college graduates and senior citizens are not cyclical economic variables, and our present monetary and fiscal policies are ill able to absorb them into the marketplace.

A new economic policy should be implemented that puts people first, rather than some place down the balance sheet.[8] Rather than focusing on our scarce national resources, we should begin to concentrate on what Wirtz has called our boundless resource, human capital. Starting from a fuller identification of individual and social needs, a new economic model would center on services rather than on products. Private enterprise would take a giant step forward as new industries are created.

7. G. William Miller, "The Not Impossible Goal: Full Employment and Price Stability," address at the 50th Annual Traffic Club of Pittsburgh, Pennsylvania, January 27, 1977.

8. *Interface: Growing Initiatives Between the Corporation and Campus Toward Greater Mutual Understanding* (New York: Council for Financial Aid to Education, 1977), pp. 18–19.

Without detracting from our present industries, such a move would add new competitive ventures to American commerce and stimulate greater collaboration among the different groups which are suffering under the present system.

Exemplary efforts

Two current collaborative efforts may be taken as examples of what might be done: those of the National Manpower Institute (NMI) and the National Urban League's Black Executive Exchange Program (BEEP).

The NMI has recently established a national consortium of work-education councils representing twenty one communities from Bethel, Maine, to Seattle, Washington, in which community leaders from business, education, labor, government, civic groups, and service agencies come together to examine the school-to-work and work-to-school transition needs of youth and young adults. The wisdom of the current lock-step progression of taking twelve, fourteen, or sixteen years of schooling all at one sitting is being questioned in all these communities. While no two communities have identical education-work agendas, they share a healthy interest in examining the conventional wisdom about the nature of youth and young adult employment. In many cases, they are coming to recognize that the responsibility for preparing young people to assume adult economic roles and responsibilities is a joint one, shared by business, postsecondary education, and other social institutions. In sixteen of the twenty-one communities, top-level decision-makers from four-year public and private colleges are involved on the councils, brought there by the realization that the problem now extends beyond high school drop-outs to include a sizable proportion of their own graduates.[9]

The Black Executive Exchange Program, sponsored by the National Urban League, also involves cooperation between business and academe. Fifty-four predominantly black colleges and universities are inviting business and professional men and women from both the public and the private sector to serve as visiting professors on a rotating basis, lecturing for two consecutive days in credit-bearing courses. So far,

9. *Work-Education Councils: Profiles of 21 Collaborative Efforts* (Washington: National Manpower Institute, 1977).

representatives from some 350 corporations have participated in this program, which has four goals:

- to augment college courses with actual industry-related experiences;
- to supplment the teaching resources of the faculty with those of business executives;
- to provide students with role models; and
- to establish and maintain a free-flowing exchange between industry and academe.[10]

A new role for trustees

American business and American higher education are both undergoing a crisis of confidence. Educators are being forced to look more closely at virtually all their assumptions about teaching and learning. Increasingly, they find themselves being judged by the same criteria as business managers. While it might help to have someone with the skills of a symphony conductor to coordinate more effectively the world of academe and the world of work, the resulting music would still not sound very good because something is terribly wrong with the way the score is written. We need some new economic models that put people first.

Many businessmen are pleased to be associated with college and university boards; I currently serve as a trustee for two colleges. One of the special virtues of a governing board is that the trustees are outsiders; they are not caught up in the premises and the process of the educational operation. They are much less likely to be prejudiced than they are to be ignorant of educational matters. This is fortunate since ignorance is a weakness more easily overcome than prejudice.

If a college education is to be made worth the investment, then trustees had better move from the outside to the inside and come to understand something of educational policy. Their responsibility should be expanded beyond the definition of broad objectives; they should also become concerned with the process of reaching those objectives, and they should make sure that the procedures in the process are initiated, maintained, and protected. In some matters, the trustees may decide to go beyond what is required by law; they may find themselves shaping social policy. In those situations where the government and the courts

10. *Interface.*

refuse to take a stand, I personally would hope that the trustees, working with academic administrators, would take a firm stand on admitting those who would probably be rejected for some very obvious historical reasons.

Such an expansion of trustee involvement will mean some stepping over onto the turf of the dean of admissions or the professor. I would hope that trustees can develop to the point where they will be able to say openly: "Our job is to perpetuate the institution in a way that contributes to the common good. We cannot meet that responsibility without becoming concerned with the educational program and its relevance to today's and tomorrow's environment."

It is a fact that many college graduates today are not very useful in the private sector. Trustees, businessmen, and educators need to make this their deepest concern. We will not have fulfilled our obligation until we know more about what goes on in, and what comes out of, our higher educational system.

AMERICAN COUNCIL ON EDUCATION

J. W. PELTASON, *President*

The American Council on Education, founded in 1918 and composed of institutions of higher education and national and regional associations, is the nation's major coordinating body for postsecondary education. Through voluntary and cooperative action, the Council provides comprehensive leadership for improving educational standards, policies, and procedures.